ABOVE
THE LINE

Center Point
Large Print

Also by Shirley MacLaine and available from Center Point Large Print:

What If . . .

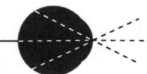

**This Large Print Book carries the
Seal of Approval of N.A.V.H.**

ABOVE THE LINE

My Wild Oats Adventure

Shirley MacLaine

CENTER POINT LARGE PRINT
THORNDIKE, MAINE

This Center Point Large Print edition is published
in the year 2016 by arrangement with Atria Books,
a division of Simon & Schuster, Inc.

The text of this Large Print edition is unabridged.
In other aspects, this book may vary
from the original edition.
Printed in the United States of America
on permanent paper.
Set in 16-point Times New Roman type.

ISBN: 978-1-68324-027-3

Library of Congress Cataloging-in-Publication Data

Names: MacLaine, Shirley, 1934– author.
Title: Above the line : my Wild oats adventure / Shirley MacLaine.
Description: Center Point Large Print edition. | Thorndike, Maine :
Center Point Large Print, 2016. | ©2016
Identifiers: LCCN 2016014161 | ISBN 9781683240273
    (hardcover : alk. paper)
Subjects: LCSH: MacLaine, Shirley, 1934- | Entertainers—United
States—Biography. | Spiritualists—United States—Biography. | Wild
oats (Motion picture) | Large type books.
Classification: LCC PN2287.M18 A3 2016b | DDC 791.4302/8092—
dc23
LC record available at http://lccn.loc.gov/2016014161

To all the below-the-line,
with love and appreciation

Some of the names and details in this account have been changed. As you read, you will understand why. The experience is my truth as I remember it.

ABOVE THE LINE

To Whom It May Concern:

You people have been pitifully amateurish, bordering on corrupt. You have been unfair in continually changing your minds. People have spent their own personal money because they know there is a schedule to meet. Yet we don't know whether the money is even there to make this movie, *Wild Oats.* Your oats are being sown in ways that are wildly unfair.

Show me the money and I'll show you my signature.

On behalf of everyone who is having a difficult time with your inability to organize even a Good Humor Bar, I'm waiting . . .

No money, no signee, no movie: only dirty laundry.

Have a nice day though.

THAT WAS the email I almost sent.

But I'm glad I didn't. The day I wrote it was the opening round of a boxing match between me and independent filmmaking. Why were we in the ring? That's what this book is about.

It isn't often that a person my age (eighty-one), with a past (this time around) of work pretty well done and a life exuberantly led, gets to experience a real-life movie while making a reel-movie movie on next to no money.

Making a movie is the most useful experience I've found for getting to know more about myself. But you don't have to be an actor or work in show business to have that experience. We're all creating our lives every day. We are the actors and writers and directors and producers and financiers of our lives. So I'd say that means that our life itself is an art, one we've chosen to take part in. It's like a movie we've chosen to make. Both need financing. Did anyone assure us when we were born that the money would be there? No. Did anyone assure me when I began *Wild Oats* that the money would be there? No. So why did I do it? Ambition? Adventure? Challenge? Fame? Because they asked me to? I'm not sure the "why" even matters now.

Is any of what we call real actually real anyway?

I realize that's a big question, and one that came back to me many times during the events I'll be sharing with you in this book. Here's a part of the answer: you've got to sow your own wild oats to find out.

Wild Oats started about five years ago. I sat at dinner in New York in the Village with two women.

I can't really remember many details about them except one was heavyset and one lived part-time in Paris. They had a script about two women who went off on an adventure . . . or was it a mother and daughter? Or was it a grandmother and granddaughter? There have been so many versions, I've forgotten them all. It was kind of a comedy—but not really that funny. I was polite but more interested in the dinner I was having. Delicious and French. *Somebody* knew what they were doing. There was a woman director involved. I don't remember if she was one of the women at dinner. Fast-forward a year . . .

I had a meeting with that director, who actually said to me, "I don't know or care how much money the movie will cost. That's not my job. I'm going to shoot the script we wrote."

I don't know where the expression "amateur night in Dixie" comes from, even though I *am* from the South and I stopped being an amateur a long time ago, at least where films are concerned. When I asked the director what the budget was, or should be, she said, "I'm not interested." She said the same thing when I asked how long the shoot would be and how much I'd be paid. When I came right out and asked, "Do you have the money to make the film?" she repeated, "I'm not interested." So by the end of the meeting, I said, "Likewise," and left.

Fast-forward one or two more years . . .

● ● ●

I have an agent named Jack Gilardi who inherited me after Mort Viner, my previous agent, died on the tennis court. Jack professes to be around seventy-eight, but he's older than me. He's from Chicago and basically trusts me, I think, because I once told Sam Giancana to f—— himself. I trust him because he trusts me. I've not changed agencies since I came to Hollywood in 1954. I know it's stylish to keep changing, but an artist's career is in a constant state of change anyway. If it's not, then you're not going for longevity. So when it came to my representation, I stayed with what I knew and trusted.

I love Jack, and vice versa, and am well aware that I'm involved with putting his grandkids through college! I can't retire. I want them to be educated. So Jack was involved with the conversations about *Wild Oats* from the beginning, and he eventually worked out the deal for me to take the part. Neither of us had a clue what we were getting into.

The original script and story was to be shot in Las Vegas (a place where the women could sow their oats). But when other states and cities started offering tax rebates and so forth to film companies, studios and screenwriters shifted their focus to saving money instead of saving scripts.

That was okay at first, but as time passed, the

budget of any movie came to trump the story. Actors realized they would be shooting wherever the biggest rebates were, and so they were always waiting for rewrites reflecting a new location. Thus, the availability of the actors continually shifted.

The *Wild Oats* script was written and rewritten for Pittsburgh, Las Vegas, New York, New Orleans, Puerto Rico, and finally, the Canary Islands.

My original costar was Jacki Weaver. Because Jacki finally took work on a television series and had to withdraw, over the next five years we at various times welcomed to the cast Kathy Bates, Jane Fonda, Bette Midler, and finally Jessica Lange.

That's just one part of what went on during the five years it took to get ready to shoot. Thanks to amateur decisions, stupid contracts, and scattered decision making, five hundred thousand dollars had been spent even before we landed in the Canary Islands.

I came across the world with Jessica. I had never met her, but when I called her, concerned about the state of the production, her words echoed in my ears: "Even if the money isn't there and we don't make the movie, they're paying for my trip to have mojitos on the beach in the Canary Islands."

That made sense to me, and besides, she liked the script. Neither of us knew who was cast with us. I gave up trying to keep track. At various times, there had been Alan Arkin, Jim Brolin, Donald Sutherland, Frank Langella, Brian Dennehy, Jon Voight, Kelsey Grammer, John Lithgow, and Christopher Walken.

I hate flying at thirty-seven thousand feet for longer than four or five hours. The trip to the Canary Islands was thirteen hours on Iberia Airlines. I realized then that Iberia Airlines must have made a deal with the producers.

The seats, however, were comfortable, and I'm glad to say weren't the pod-like structures that to me resemble nothing so much as the kind of tiny, bargain-size New York apartment that you can barely afford when you're broke. I wore my ozonizer around my neck and doused my hand wipe with more water, fit it inside my eye cover, placed it around my nose, and breathed in moist air. That always solves my problem with dry nose from air travel.

A woman representing the production company traveled with us. I will call her Miranda. She seemed sweet, attentive, and quiet. I was especially pleased with the quiet part.

Jessica was assigned a seat a few rows behind me, not within talking distance. We were both glad of that.

I read, declined booze, drank water, and contemplated why I was on the plane. Apparently, after they'd heard I hadn't made it onto the first flight that had been scheduled for me, the company on the Islands location waiting to begin shooting had placed bets as to whether I'd get on this plane.

I noticed on the way to the toilet that Jessica was studying the script and making notes. I hadn't read the thing since I'd suggested it shouldn't be about two women on an adventure but rather a mother and daughter or grand-daughter. I thought two women who were friends was too reminiscent of *Thelma and Louise*. Grandmother and granddaughter provided an opportunity for an entertaining gap in generations as they were on an adventure.

I thought the latter idea would attract more investors and younger audiences. But the producer, Tyne, stuck to the original idea. At least I thought it was the original. I couldn't remember which script I had agreed to do. There had been such drama over whether I had signed my contract that I'd overlooked the reason for making a movie at all—the script. I didn't know who was financing or who the individual investors were. Everyone involved with my "movie team" in Hollywood advised me not to go until all the money was in. I consulted my psychic friends, who were usually right. To a person they said, "Don't go until you have the money in the bank."

I got pleading emails and desperate phone calls

from the director, Andy Tennant. "Please come. Please. Please. We are here waiting for you; without you all our efforts and financial investments and creative time and energy will mean nothing."

I knew no one else who was cast except for Jessica Lange. I wondered if she knew she would be playing not only Jacki Weaver's part but also Kathy Bates's and Bette Midler's too! I called Jessica and raised my concerns once more and asked what her people were advising her. "They all say don't go," she said. "But if it doesn't work out after I'm there, I told you, I'll just drink mojitos on the beach. Who's financing, by the way—any idea?"

I said I didn't know. Neither did my agent, Jack, and neither did the director or anyone else involved. I remembered the original director saying, "The money? I'm not interested." Was I now doing the same thing? There was some talk about a millionaire who maybe owned an island or two. There was a letter stating that his money was apparently good . . . to the tune of $3.5 million.

Another producer named Michelos had maneuvered a tax and rebate deal with the Canary Islands for $2.5 million. And there were smaller investors at thirty thousand apiece.

In the course of making the movie, I came to understand that the character of an investor is the most important thing to know about him or her. After sixty years in the business, I'd never realized that the personal character of each investor was as important to the film's outcome as the characters in the movie. But then, that was what independent filmmaking had become: the art of lining up investors.

There are two businesses in this world— everybody else's business and show business. Everyone wants to be in show business, at least once. That's where the personal values and character of the investors comes in. But I don't want to get ahead of my story.

We landed in Madrid. The airport there is a twin to Rodeo Drive in Beverly Hills. All the brand-name, high-end designers are represented in luxurious shops that beckoned us simply to browse.

No one from the production met us in Madrid to shepherd us through to the next leg of the trip: three and a half hours to the Canary Islands. But Miranda spoke Spanish, so we were fine.

When I noticed so many of my fellow travelers to the Islands were German, I couldn't help but reflect on the alliance between Hitler and Franco of Spain during the Spanish Civil War, a rehearsal for the Second World War. Traveling has always been a history lesson for me, making real what is otherwise a printed chapter in a book.

Exhausted, I nonetheless wondered why we

hadn't gone through customs or the Spanish version of TSA. I became markedly aware that fame and power in Spain made a person exempt from such invasions of privacy. I guessed the days of royalty and dictatorship still had a lot of sway over what the common man goes through.

On Iberia Airlines to the Canary Islands, first class had three seats across but the middle seat on every row was empty. I found out later it was empty "to ensure the comfort of the seats on either side." There were people turned away at the gate because the flight was full.

I noticed an advertisement for the airline: "Only Iberia Can Fly Your Clients to the Lost Continent of Atlantis." Intriguing. My mind swirled into metaphysical mode. I'd researched this place before I'd set out on this adventure, and I'd learned that many people believed that the Canary Islands were the remnants of Atlantis. The ocean I could see out the airplane window was the same one into which parts of the continent of Atlantis had supposedly sunk.

When we landed at Gran Canaria and I disembarked, I was stunned at what greeted me—a *wheelchair* and an attending medic! I was told later that intense discussion and deliberation had gone into the size and make of that wheelchair. I was also told they had scheduled regular naps for me during the stay. Frankly, I laughed, but out of embarrassment. I'd been pressured to come to the set now in order to reassure nervous investors of the start date of the shoot—and yet I was to arrive in a wheelchair with a doctor? What did eighty years old mean to these people anyway?

The drive from the airport to the hotel played a big part in a scene in the movie. I expected palm trees and wafting ocean breezes. The landscape included palm trees all right, but they protruded out of hills that had been carved into and hacked away. Although part of Spain, the Canary Islands are just sixty miles off the coast of Morocco, and what I was seeing looked more like the Moroccan desert than Spain. Everywhere the land was barren, and many of the hillsides were slate and rock that seemed to have been mined. I could see palm trees in the sand in the distance . . . but the landscape was not at all what I had expected.

Ron Howard had shot *In the Heart of the Sea* there for months the previous year; with their tax rebates, the islands have become a favorite place to save money on a shoot—particularly if it doesn't matter exactly what it looks like because your production is going to use a lot of green screen.

As we approached the hotel, the environment shifted. First I noticed a wave of shops— electronics equipment, food markets, malls, hairdressers. Then, straight ahead loomed the resort hotel. It was the gigantic Lopesan, with well-tended gardens, circular driveways for buses and limos, Spanish-style architecture with vaulted exterior walkways over which palm trees swayed in a gentle breeze.

I got out of the car and immediately spotted the high-end dress shops that would serve not only the German tourists but provide much of our own wardrobe for the film. After all, the women Jessica and I were playing were supposed to be on an adventure, leaving their past—and their hometown style—behind. I remembered the fittings I had had a week before. Dozens of off-the-rack garments, which the costume designer had paid for herself since the funding wasn't quite in place. Jesus . . .

I entered the ultra-luxurious lobby wondering who was paying for all this. That's when I realized the hotel and everything in it would be "product placement" in the film. But what if the film never got made? Who would be responsible for the bill we would all rack up? (The bill for the hotel rooms and all the food and drinks turned out to be the cost of a movie by itself. But no getting ahead of my story.)

I was greeted by hotel staff as if I were the Queen of England. In the elevator to the sixth floor, I was recognized by a group of German tourists. I guessed the sales of my films in Germany must have still been pretty respectable. (Money for films these days comes from selling the distribution rights to foreign territories.) \

Most of the international territories would fund me in a comedy or a musical. Our script had some laughs, but I was quite sure that there was no money put aside for things like postproduction music. But I'm getting ahead of myself again!

I was ushered into a large, luxurious suite that had a view of the ocean far off in the distance. It seemed too quiet. I didn't hear the waves, but then how could I from this distance? Below me, there was a massive patio full of tables and chairs and lounging couches and waiters and bulging German tourists eating munchies and drinking caipirinhas (a Brazilian cocktail to die for) as they breathed in the ocean air and relaxed. Their vacations ranged from two weeks to a full month. This was to be the view from my window every day.

The hotel manager led me through the sitting room into my bedroom and bath. There were sweet-smelling candles everywhere (a gift from the producer Michelos), snacks, fruit, and flowers. Very nice. The bedroom also overlooked the ocean and the sprawling patio of tourists below. I noticed two smallish outdoor stages in the midst of the patio. I wondered what would happen upon these stages, but didn't ask the manager. Big mistake.

Adjacent to the bedroom was a luxurious marble bathroom, which was pretty to look at but meant only one thing to me: I was sure to fall on the slippery-when-wet floor. Anticipating this, I asked for rubber mats to be placed clear across the bathroom floor and into the shower. Such a request was not very graciously received by the management, but they did it anyway. One fall and I'd have needed that wheelchair for sure. I refrained from asking how the shower worked. (It looked like the cockpit of a spaceship.) I figured it would be good exercise for my brain to take the time to figure it out myself, as long as I didn't lose my balance in the process.

Someone unpacked for me (since I was the queen who would provide the management with product placement).

After I'd freshened up (but still gotten no sleep), Andy the director called and asked me to join everyone on the patio for a drink. On the way down in the elevator, I found out something new about myself. Traveling to unfamiliar places always puts me in touch with what I don't yet know about myself. This time I realized I needed to be more aware of the limitations of my memory capacity. As soon as I'd left my room and walked down the hall, I couldn't remember my room number or even what floor it was on. I was confused when I tried to call room service or the front desk from a phone in the hallway. I had become used to my cell phone (no easy task), but were the phones in hotels landlines? There didn't seem to be an operator on the other end.

What if I really needed to speak to a human being? I understood that technology had taken over the world (particularly for wealthy people), but only in that moment did I grasp that I hadn't paid enough attention to all the newfangled means of communication. And when I got in the elevator and realized I was unsure which button to press for the lobby, I waited for someone else to get in and push the right one for me. Maybe I *did* need that wheelchair at the airport.

Whenever a new faculty is developed into being, an old one loses its force and precision.

Memory is nearer to the deep
foundations laid by Nature
in humankind than is the
power of reason.

WHEN I finally reached the Grand Patio below, I said a big hello to everyone, sat down, and was introduced to my first caipirinha cocktail. When I realized that that drink made me feel better about *everything,* I knew I was in big trouble.

Everyone was drinking. I tried to absorb who they all were and what they did. Andy was clearly in charge. I had never worked with him and had only met him once before, at a lunch overlooking the Pacific in Malibu. He claims that within half an hour I knew more about him than his wife. So what else is new? Bobby Harling, whom I met and became friends with on *Steel Magnolias* (he wrote it), had worked with Andy on *Sweet Home Alabama* and told me he liked and trusted him. "Plus, he makes hits," said Bobby.

During the preproduction insanity, I had strongly urged that we postpone the shoot until we were completely ready and fully financed (ha!). The producer, Tyne, had been so inexperienced and had so little professional assistance from lawyers that financing and deals and contracts kept changing. It truly sounded like a colossal mess to me, as it did to Andy, but there was something about the script, me, the location, and the magic of the movie itself that propelled him forward. I'll never forget the sound of his voice, the vibration, the frequency of his emotion, when he said with total conviction and certainty, "We are making this movie. Nothing will stop me. We can't postpone for any reason. We are going forward. *I am making this movie now.*" It was almost mystically imbued. That one speech had convinced me to sign the contract and get on the plane. It was to propel me through the whole experience—the utterly assured sound of his voice.

Andy would say I was the reason *Oats* got made. I say he was the reason. I didn't learn until later that several times, after sounding so confident, he had almost booked himself on a flight home. Basically, though, I think I was there because anything that smacked of an ancient truth that was familiar to me was a magnet. I was to learn later that I was right.

So we sat around on the patio mingling and chatting about this movie that we each were crazy enough to be a part of. I met people from wardrobe, hair, makeup, the director of photography, assistant directors, line producers, accountants. They all said, "Thank you for getting on the plane." As the evening went on, I came to see that in this particular situation, I was more than a lead actor in a film. Why had I created this reality for myself? Then it hit me. The movie itself was important, but the *making* of it was the crucial adventure. And as all the inherent implications of that sank in, I realized that I was emotionally committed to this film. I was deeply involved with getting it made but somehow still neutral as to its potential financial, professional, and critical results. Whatever happened after we finished was supposed to.

Was this quietly engaged state of being what Buddha and Nelson Mandela were talking about? Was a low-budget, independent movie made where the tax credits and rebates were good the fitting location in time and space for me to learn a profound lesson about the value of art versus materialism? Of course it was. We were on islands that were formed from the remnants of Atlantis, a civilization which, according to researchers specializing in esoteric matters, had lasted for eight hundred fifty thousand years. As legend has it, Atlantis sank because of the Atlantean people's addiction to high-level technology and materialism. Of course we would succeed because we had none of that! Yeah, right.

In addition to having past-life memories of my time on the advanced continent of Atlantis, I had read whatever writings or research I could find about it. The people inhabiting the islands today accepted as fact that their land had been part of the ancient continent. They hadn't read Plato or Socrates or any of the great Greek writers who referred to its existence. But in private, most everyone I met said that they believed the "myth" of Atlantis to be fact. They said they could feel it in the air and the ocean. What such a belief meant to them was not clear. Nor was it to me . . . until I became more involved in the production of a movie.

In the 1800s, mystic Madame Blavatsky claimed that she learned about Atlantis from Tibetan gurus; a century later, psychic Edgar Cayce claimed that Atlantis was an ancient, highly evolved civilization powered by crystals. Plato in his *Critias* and *Timaeus* dialogues left such a convincing description of Atlantis that many scholars doubted his information could have been imagined.

In his book *Frauds, Myths, and Mysteries: Science and Pseudoscience in Archaeology*, professor Ken Feder summarizes the story: "A technologically sophisticated but morally bankrupt evil empire—Atlantis—attempts world domination by force. The only thing standing in its way is a relatively small group of spiritually pure, morally principled, and incorruptible people—the ancient Athenians. Overcoming overwhelming odds, the Athenians were able to defeat their far more powerful adversary simply through the force of their spirit." It sounded familiar to me. Plato's Atlantean dialogues are essentially an ancient Greek version of *Star Wars*.

Plato, however, is crystal clear about where Atlantis is: "For the ocean there was at that time navigable; for in front of the mouth which you Greeks call, as you say, 'the Pillars of Hercules' there lay an island which was larger than Libya and Asia together." In other words, it lies in the Atlantic Ocean beyond the Pillars of Hercules (i.e., the Straits of Gibraltar, at the mouth of the Mediterranean).

In *Critias*, Plato wrote of Atlantis's architecture, engineering, and ceremonies in great detail. According to Plato, one of the greatest splendors of Atlantis was the palace compound located in the heart of its capital. It was ringed by three canals. Plato remarked, "As each king received it from his predecessor, he added to its adornment and did all he could to surpass the king before him, and finally they made of it an abode amazing to behold for the magnitude and beauty of its workmanship. The visitors passed through a wall of brass, a wall of tin, and a wall of copper. White and black and red stone was quarried from the native rock." He also wrote that the wealth they possessed was so immense that the like had never been seen before in any royal house, nor will ever easily be seen again. I wished we had some of that money for our production. But of course, their materialism led to their homeland's destruction.

Plato stated that the Atlanteans appeared to be superlatively fair and blessed, yet they were filled with lawless ambition and power. Sounded a lot like Hollywood to me. The Atlanteans started valuing material wealth above goodness and morality, and that's where they went wrong. Definitely Hollywood. Plato said, "The portion of divinity within them was now becoming faint and weak through being oftentimes blended with a large measure of mortality." The Atlanteans were unable to bear the burden of their possessions. So, "there occurred portentous earthquakes and floods, and one grievous day and night befell them when . . . the island of Atlantis . . . was swallowed up by the sea and vanished." Hollywood and California? Plato doubted that any sign of the lost land would ever be found. "The ocean at that spot has now become impassable and unsearchable."

Ancient memories are some of our most prominent mental functions.

ON THAT first night on the remnants of Atlantis, cast and crew all convened for a sumptuous dinner at a restaurant adjacent to the hotel. I wondered who was footing the bill for this.

As I was enjoying my caipirinha, a woman sat down next to me, turned, and looked into my eyes. I nearly fell from my chair because her dark eyes pierced my brain and literally shrank my soul! They were so desperate, so insistent . . . frankly, slightly insane. I don't think I've ever had such a reaction to the eyes of another human being.

She said, "Thank you for getting on the plane." Others at the table saw my recoiling reaction but went on with their drinks. I didn't know who she was, this woman who looked into my eyes with such piercing intensity. She hadn't said her name. I leaned across the table and surreptitiously asked Andy, "Who is this woman next to me?"

He looked at me as though I had no brains. "That's Tyne," he said.

In every endeavor in show business—or maybe any business (I've never known any other)—I've found one consistent, sad truth. Because of the emotionality of our business, and because during production we need to become a family to pull off the make-believe, there seems to be a necessity of having one person on set to hate. When the consensus lands on that one person, the frustrations of everyone find a target. Without that target we seem unable to balance our anger, our love for our work, our impatience with time and each other. Because of her amateurness, her insistence on being there, and the colossal financial mess the production was in, Tyne did become the person to hate. No one wanted to talk to her or even acknowledge her existence except to focus their frustration on what they believed *she* was responsible for.

I hadn't remembered those eyes, and frankly, I was glad for that. I went on talking to other people, and Tyne made no attempt to engage me in further conversation.

The dinner was nice, the pizza delicious, and the caipirinhas a lifesaver. Nick the AD (assistant director) walked me back to the hotel. I knew I had to get some sleep. But how, with all the noise coming from the patio below my room? A band played so loud, you could have heard it in Madrid. I gratefully turned on CNN. I am a news freak and feel more grounded if I know what's happening in other parts of the world.

I undressed, walked on the rubber mats to the shower. No hot water. Got clean with cold water anyway and went to bed.

I hate the technology of my iPad. However, the app that I appreciate more than any other is the white noise with the owl looking out. The band played on, but the white sound from my owl app nearly covered it.

The next morning Miranda helped me put the right plugs into the right sockets so that I had my cell phone, iPad, and Canary Islands cell phone all juiced up. My bed was where the lines of communication connected. I felt like execution by electrocution was certain to be next.

She ordered breakfast for me. Scrambled eggs and decaf latte. The eggs were so fluffy, I put raw sugar on top and made a dessert for breakfast. On an accompanying tray with my coffee were crunchy cracker cookies with a hint of sugar.

I have been addicted to sugar all my life. Dancing in shows and rehearsals left me little time for good meals. I felt the sugar give me energy, so began to rely on it. I will get into what sugar does to the human body later. It is truly a weapon of mass destruction . . . and it came from the Canary Islands.

After breakfast I went into an adjacent hotel room that had been outfitted as a makeup and hair sanctuary. Since the two leading characters in the script had makeovers when they arrived at the Canary Islands resort area, it seemed to me that my character (Eva) should have hair for home and a new hairstyle for her vacation. I thought gray hair for home and red for her new life. Because I knew there was no money, I'd brought with me all the false hair and wigs I had worn in sixty years of making movies. The Hollywood hair filled a wheelbarrow! The only hair I didn't have was gray. The hairdresser said a friend of his could shop for it in Madrid and give it to someone who was coming in a few days. Fine.

The makeup artist, Mariló, was married to the director of photography, José Luis Alcaine. Alcaine was Pedro Almodóvar's DP and is famous in show business for his skill at photographing women. Most female stars would rather have him on a one-week shoot than a husband full-time. I agree. He is meticulous with his lighting and moves his seventy-four-year-old frame around the set with a limp. The first time I looked at the dailies of me and Jessica, I thought, *The critics are going to want to know who our plastic surgeon is!* I actually put my vanity aside and wondered if we looked too good for the truth. Alcaine said he would fix it later in postproduction. "Fix it in post" has become a protector against whatever you are afraid of— lighting, editing, ADR (voice separation from image), performance defects, even a lackluster script. You can rewrite a script by the way you edit it in postproduction.

I was determined to deal with my wrinkling neck and not get plastic surgery. So we used a face-lift tape which would then be secured underneath my wig. If I had a headache by lunch, that would be my problem, and it was. My skin and ears itched from the pulling. I should have let him "fix it in post."

The wardrobe, off the racks of the tourist shops, was perfect for my character in the film. The costumer herself, Lena, was experienced and bright. She had also read my book *The Camino* and wanted to know what I was really like.

The weather was beautiful, the people nice, the accommodations wonderful. And now we just had to make the movie—and get a bit more money to do it.

One of my specialties is asking people questions and finding out what's really going on. In this case it was more difficult than usual. Nobody really wanted me to know how desperate the situation was. Movie people are as silent and closed as tombs when they want to be.

In any case, I was impressed with Katy, the second AD who would give us our calls and try to keep a modicum of organization despite frequent miscommunication between the Spanish and the Americans on the crew. She was also honest. She had wanted to leave a few times because of the lack of money but stuck around to meet and talk to me. She had great respect for our line producer, Bret, and the AD, Nick, and how professionally they were prepping the film.

When she told me that Bret had put ten thousand dollars of his own money into the budget to pay for some cars one day, I understood how desperate the situation really was. And, by her telling me, I understood how much she trusted me. The first and second assistant directors had been warned by their union (the Directors Guild) that they should quit. A bond company needs to sign off on a production so that unions will allow their members to work, and we were not bonded. A woman named Amy from the bond company was there to determine whether she would give her okay to proceed. Members of the crew had not been paid for a few weeks, but according to Spanish union rules, they were not allowed to revolt for another week. However, they were not getting any per diem either and so were feeding themselves and covering other daily expenses out of their own pockets.

Jesus . . . no wonder all my psychic friends and business acquaintances had advised me to stay away.

Why *was* I here?

My interest in past lives and ancient civilizations has been a sustaining entertainment for me all my life. I had my first past-life recall when I was about seven. My family was on a history trip relating to Virginia. I stood on a hill, and suddenly I felt I had a rifle in my arms. I knew I had been a soldier at another time and place on that same hill in Virginia. I'll never forget that memory recognition. I have had others in many of the countries in which I've traveled. In fact, my life has been an entertainment of recall, so to speak. I believe that is why I've never questioned the truth that I have lived before and will do so again. I did not know that the Canary Islands were thought to be the remnants of Atlantis until Iberia Airlines advertised it. So when I arrived, my answer to "Why am I here?" seemed clear!

All of Earth's ancient peoples share the tradition of a great flood during which a civilization was destroyed by a catastrophe: a combination of flood, earthquakes, and volcanic eruptions. I wondered if Atlantis was the first tribe of humans to build a so-called civilization. And was Adam an allegory of the first man, or was Ad-Am the first civilized tribe? Did the Bible or the Torah really describe Adam and Eve as the first humans, and if so, how did they become human?

Researchers say that the Canary Islands are the tops of Atlantis's tallest mountains and that Atlantis was a highly evolved group of humans and star beings that lived many years in balanced harmony of light and used crystal grids around the Earth to spread knowledge and to communicate.

Information about Atlantis comes from many ancient texts: the Mayan, the Chaldean king list, the Egyptian records well into the prehistoric period of "the Reign of the Gods," the Mahabharata and other Hindu ancient texts, the Incas of Peru. I've often wondered who the "gods" were.

The Spanish conquerors of the Canary Islands found that the natives, called Guanches, were surprised to learn that other people had survived the disaster that had flooded their world and had left them isolated on islands that were once the tops of the high mountains of their former homeland. Plato had written, "When the 'gods' purge the Earth with a deluge of water . . . yon herdsmen and shepherds on the mountains are the survivors." The Guanches were said to have been white-skinned, often with blond hair, very tall, and of a type now catalogued as the Cro-Magnon race that existed some thirty-five thousand years ago.

Christopher Columbus possessed a number of maps showing Atlantis spelled in various ways and located just adjacent to where the Canary Islands are now. The Spaniards who reached the New World spoke of how the Native Americans talked of the ancient white gods who came in flying boats and brought them civilization. These gods had promised to return and bring other gods to continue their teaching of civilization.

We know what happened to the Aztecs and Incas when the Spanish landed with Cortés.

Walking, living, and experiencing the energy of the Canary Islands, I found myself wanting more information about how humans became humans and who those gods were who came in sky boats.

ADJUSTING TO jet lag is a process I've never been good at. I had not slept for four days, and there seemed to be no quiet anywhere in the hotel until four in the morning. Adding to my frustration was the difficulty I was having getting basic information. I long for clarity when I ask questions. But the young people who'd been hired as production assistants were not pros, so it was on-the-job training for most of them.

What really drove me crazy, though, was the habit I noticed among many of the Spanish PAs of answering a question with a question. For example, I might ask someone what time I was going to be needed on set the next day.

"What time is the rehearsal call tomorrow?" I'd ask.

"You want to know what time the rehearsal call is?" they'd reply.

"Yes."

"What time can you be there?"

"No," I'd say, "what time did they tell you to tell me to be there?"

"Did someone call you and tell you what time?"

"No, I'm asking you if you got a time for me to be there."

"You're asking me if I got a call for you?"

"Yes."

"Was someone supposed to call you?"

"No, I don't think so. Anyway, do you have an answer as to when I'm supposed to rehearse tomorrow?"

Then the inevitable, "I'll check."

At the end of every conversation and in reply to any question was "I'll check." It was as though no one trusted what they had heard with their own ears. Was it an inherited trait from so many years of feeling insecure under a royal monarch and then under Franco's dictatorship? I got so frustrated that I took to purposely confusing whomever I asked a question of. For example:

"What time is my rehearsal call?" I'd ask.

"You want to know what time your rehearsal call is?" they'd answer.

"Who said anything about a rehearsal call?"

They'd look confused and say, "Didn't you ask what time your rehearsal call is?" they'd ask.

I'd say, "I'll check."

Nobody got the game I was playing. They just went on being confused.

The weather, however, was continually beautiful, the food excellent if you knew what to order, and the caipirinhas the best thing that had happened to me in a long time.

Andy was confident, not afraid of me, knew comedy, rhythm, and was totally in charge. The crew was terrific, the shopped wardrobe beautiful. I found some beautiful Italian boots in a German shop.

I still didn't know what men were cast in the film. I only knew who couldn't wait any longer and had moved on to take other work. Then, out of nowhere, Billy Connolly arrived ready to shoot. I did not even know he had been cast! His personality was the driest, most intelligent, unencumbered comic mix I had ever encountered. I knew many smart people who considered him one of the best comic actors in the business, but until I met him, I had never understood why. He was supposed to play my con-man lover, which seemed off base to me, but he made me laugh so hard, I nearly developed a herniated disk. We had a love scene together, which I couldn't have imagined even on another planet. He told me quite openly about his childhood. His father left the family. His mother had many boyfriends, who would often kick him out of his own house. He spent many years traumatized and confused, which he must have used to perfect his comedy. Was the best and truest comedy really based on deep tragedy, as we are so often told?

Was this the lesson of Robin Williams's suicide? As I write this now, I am still unable to process the tragedy of his action. Hanging himself by his belt? What was he trying to tell us? Did he take his life so dramatically because he wanted to emphasize the seriousness of what caused his depression? And what was that? Drugs, alcohol, money, work?

The figures on suicide in this country are truly troubling. Eight hundred thousand suicides per year, one every forty seconds. Has our technology preempted our ability to fulfill our need for human intimacy and personal communication? When I looked around the restaurant at night, I saw people were texting each other across the dinner table rather than simply speaking to one another.

Most of Robin's humor was based on his experience with drugs, booze, and his tragic, truthful outlook on life. At the root of all his humor was his recognition of what had become tragic. That seems to be the prerequisite of laughter. All humor is gallows humor. Has life itself become the belt we live with?

Do you feed your soul, or your body,
or the place in between—your mind?

THERE SEEMED to be little to no communication between the American and Spanish crew members. There had been five years of trouble just to get us to this point, many lawyers, countless conference calls, two directors, ten scripts, seven proposed locations, and of course, even now—no money.

I had a driver about six ten who seemed very nice and protective. His name was Manuel. His constant concern: "Do I do a good job?" He always had his arm out for me to lean on so I wouldn't lose my balance. I had broadcast to everyone involved in the movie: "I'm not afraid of anything much—except falling." They all took notice. Even the four-eleven, ninety-five-pound assistant put out her arm to ensure my balance when I walked by.

We waited about a week for money to arrive from the investors . . . Nothing.

Jessica's schedule was a problem because she had to complete her work on our picture so she could report to *American Horror Story* in New Orleans on a specific and unmovable date. It was in her contract. So the morning after we arrived, she shot her first scene. It was a comic love scene with a young man her character had picked up in a restaurant. It involved shoving him up against the wall and jumping on him because her husband had left her and she was free to do all the outrageous things she had repressed until then. I heard she was funny and abandoned and the scene worked. I was in my room trying to sleep.

Off set, Jessica was sweet, a pro, not social, beautiful, intense, and a brilliant dramatic actress. I liked her a lot and assured her she *would* be funny. We had many conversations about the men in our lives, which will certainly not be shared here.

The man cast as her lover was supposed to have been the real-life lover of one of the investors. But, it seemed, because the money had not been delivered, he was eighty-sixed. Axed. Fired. He wasn't right for the part anyway. Andy instead cast someone who was, and he traveled overnight the night before from Los Angeles to do the scene.

The production office was apparently chaotic. I didn't know many details because Andy didn't want me to know. Above-the-line (creative) people are supposed to be unburdened with the truth—particularly unpleasant financial truth. So, in effect, we were now shooting with a crew who weren't being paid but did it anyway.

Our producer, Michelos, had racked up his own credit card to pay for food, rooms, drinks, and accessories. If the film shut down, he would be liable for over a million dollars because the products he'd bartered for placement in the film wouldn't have anywhere to be placed!

We all waited every night to see if there was enough money to shoot the next day. On one occasion the chaos in the production office revolved around a desperate attempt to raise four thousand dollars or so to pay the cabdrivers' union the following morning. At midnight someone called us and said, "We got the money for the drivers. Report to set at six a.m." I don't know who contributed the money. But I suspect it was our accountant, who dearly loved the project and would do what she could afford to keep it going. I learned later that Mandy, our accountant, had put over a hundred thousand on her credit card, and the Spanish producer whose company had hired the crew and equipment had spent four hundred thousand dollars of her own money. But after the cabdrivers debacle, the inevitable happened. We shut down.

I was relegated to a happier and more joyous pastime—watching the news. ISIS was executing people who didn't believe in their version of God, Iraq was falling under their command, babies and women were dying by the side of the road, dire flooding was taking place in California, what wasn't flooding was burning up, Obama was facing potential impeachment, Israelis and Palestinians were busy killing each other over their versions of God, and Ebola was wiping out West Africa just sixty miles from where we were trying to make a movie. . . . Atlantis, anyone?

The development of memory in humans led to enormous individual power.
Which led to exercising the power solely for oneself. Which led to ambition, which became selfishness and
resulted in the misuse of life forces. The Atlanteans' misuse of life forces had incredible consequences. Such power over Nature led to self-service, materialism, decadence, and decay.

Mankind learned to make use of
Natural Forces without being
conscious of their Divine origin.
We were unaware of the
Divine Order of Things.

Blavatsky said, "The whole Globe is convulsed periodically; and has been so convulsed, since the appearance of the First Race . . . four times.

"The continents perish in turn by fire and water: either through earthquakes and volcanic eruptions, or by sinking and the great displacement of waters. Our continents have to perish owing to the former cataclysmic process."

Seven hundred and fifty thousand years before the present, an advanced civilization existed that would program its own demise through its diminishing sense of morality, its out-of-control high-level technology, its lack of spiritual life, and its chronic addiction
to materialism. The Greek historians suggested that such cataclysmic events occurred once every ten thousand years. We are now, since 2012,
at the end of one of these ten-thousand-year periods.

I WENT shopping with Miranda. Miranda's job was basically to be the social people-pleaser who helped the producer raise money for our picture. Not going too well. She was, however, very nice and efficient, could put up with my impatience and needling professionalism, and became my assistant because the young nonpro girl who answered questions with questions didn't work out. Miranda was an expert in what to order from the restaurant and what buttons to push in the room to do it. She told me about the nude beach and the nude gay beach, where it was, and how to get there in case at my age I was interested. I would wait on that one.

Miranda was ambitious. She was quite lovely-looking too. I couldn't ascertain what she really wanted out of life—to produce movies? To act in them? To raise money only? To travel mainly? And she gossiped a lot, so I didn't need to go far to find out what was going on. She gossiped with an agenda, meaning there was usually a reason she was saying what she was saying. She was ultra-nice with me, even when I had a temperamental meltdown while tearing my wig (which was stuck) and yelling that there was no hot water and why did they take my rubber mats away, and why the hell did they say they had the money when they didn't?

She said, "I'm not sure I can do this job." She was honest and right, and I was miserable even though the shopping was great, the weather beautiful, and the caipirinhas strong.

Every night the band below my spacious and luxurious suite began their sets at 7:30. They went until 11:30. They were loud (with speakers) and could be heard for miles around and out to the ocean. I knew I would never make it with that band, despite my iPad white noise turned up to nosebleed. I asked for a room on the street side of the hotel and even asked Miranda to switch with me. She didn't want to do that. But Michelos, the producer who was racking up his credit cards, said he would. "My brain is so numb from the problems and I haven't slept in months anyway. I'd be glad to switch." He then moved into the pricey holocaust of noise pollution and I moved to his suite.

When I walked into his nice but smallish suite and saw his belongings, which hadn't yet been moved, I understood what he must have been going through. His suits were perfectly lined up in the closet, his toiletries in geometric lines, his accessories stacked atop one another in such a fashion that everything belied the fact that someone was living there. This kind of man was in charge of the heartbreaking chaos that he had dedicated so much to? Must be a karmic lesson, I thought. In fact, the entire shebang must be a karmic lesson for all of us.

Jessica was off after three days of shooting. She went back to her family who had a cabin in the hills of Minnesota. I couldn't imagine taking another plane ride. Although since most of my scenes were with Jessica, I didn't work much when Jessica didn't, and I thought seriously of going to Morocco, which was right off the coast sixty miles away. I had enjoyed it so much when I was there forty years ago. Had it changed? Had the Arabs become militant? Was the souk I had shopped in still there? Would I ever cross the Sahara on a camel, as I nearly did with a friend of mine who had since died? How adventurous I had always been, with almost no concern for my safety, health, or circumstance.

I thought about going to New York to see some Broadway shows. However, I heard that the production office would freak out because they feared I might not return.

I decided to stay closer to "home" and go to La Palma, another island in the Canary chain. I wanted to visit the Caldera, a volcano that had erupted years before. I remembered seeing a documentary on the Caldera in which some of the top geologists in the world had concluded that the Caldera was dangerously top-heavy and was someday going to collapse, taking half the island with it. The geologists said it could then set up a tidal wave—a tsunami which would rise to more than one thousand feet, cross the Atlantic, rising higher and higher, and when the Atlantic tsunami hit North America, it would take out most of the eastern seaboard of the United States! The geologists had concluded that this wasn't an *if,* but a *when.* Would Atlantis rise again to remind us of why it had sunk in the first place? Materialism and technology replacing spirituality.

THE LOCAL plane to La Palma was a scene out of someone else's bad movie. There was no air-conditioning, the seating was first come/first served, and there were not even enough seats for those who came first, expecting to be served. Sunburned tourists were everywhere, and no one except for me seemed to mind the conditions. We were going to see the volcano. Given the holiday mood, I gathered I was the only one who had heard that it was now going to collapse in on itself, take half of the island of La Palma with it, and cause a tsunami that would destroy the east coast of the United States, fulfilling a prediction by the great Edgar Cayce.

On the plane with me was a very important, and rather good-looking, person. I had met him on the veranda where they served caipirinhas the day before. I understood from Miranda that he was Dominick Hollins, the millionaire who had agreed to put $3.5 million into our film. He had come to check us out before he closed on his investment.

He'd sauntered toward me on the veranda and seemed a little bit drunk. He sat down and said,

"How the fuck are ya? I'm from Virginia too. Call me Trey." I was startled, but I thought, *People with that much money can pretty much behave any way they want, I guess.*

"Charlottesville and North Carolina," he went on.

I had noticed he bit his nails down to the quick and his energy was all over the place. *Jesus,* I thought, *is he reliable?* Then he said, "Listen, I was out by the lighthouse in front of the hotel last night and I saw a UFO. I heard a voice say, 'Speak to Shirley MacLaine and tell her.'"

Oh boy . . .

"So we have a lot to talk about," he continued.
Okay.

Miranda blinked slightly.

"I know they are really here," he said. "Right?"

I nodded and asked him what he wanted to know specifically about the subject. After all, our entire movie depended on his going through with his investment.

"They told me you have much to teach me and many others. Yes?"

I had given him what I hoped was a mysterious smile. He ordered a drink. He asked me further superficial questions about UFOs, but I really was interested in whether he actually saw one. We were in Atlantis, after all! Were the Gods in sky boats really ETs?

Then he'd switched to telling me about his personal relationship with one of the producers, a man, and how they shared a love of music. "I'm a record producer. I have a big record company in L.A. I have to get back tomorrow. The workers play when the boss is away." Wasn't that quote about mice and a cat? He was engaging, especially when I got the idea he was withholding his $3.5 million until he saw fit to let it go.

I'd told him I was going to La Palma the next day because without money we couldn't shoot anyway. I described the Caldera and the stories surrounding it. He said, "Fuck yeah. I can put off leaving for one day." Hmm.

He ordered another drink. He talked about his Southern family, particularly his mother, but never mentioned his investment or his millions. I didn't like being around his energy, so after a little while longer, I begged off and told him that Miranda and I would see him tomorrow, we'd make a reservation for him on the plane. Fine. Cut to the next day . . .

We were on the plane waiting to land in La Palma. Trey seemed anxious but not excessively so, especially given the plane we were on. Upon landing, Miranda realized we needed a car and a driver, or a cab, or some form of transportation to get us to the Caldera. Trey turned to her and said, "I thought this was all arranged." She sheepishly lowered her head. There was a mini argument/discussion about where the mountain was. I didn't participate. I was too engrossed in the interplay to be goal-oriented.

Somehow they made a decision to rent a car and depend upon street signs to get us to the mountain. We took off.

Immediately, there was tension. The street signs were in Spanish, which Trey couldn't understand and Miranda didn't know how to obey. We ended up in a small village that was nowhere near the mountain. Trey and Miranda quietly began to bicker. I sat in the back of the car, silent. I was intrigued. Neither was able to be decisive about what to do next.

I saw a tour bus. "Ask the tour bus driver if he's going to the Caldera. Then let's follow him." That's what we did. But Trey and Miranda still needed to argue.

"I don't like being stressed out," said Miranda.

"I'm sorry I made you stressed out," said Trey. Silence. Then more aggressively, Trey said, "I'm really sorry I made you stressed out and mad." Then, as though to provoke Miranda, "I don't like it either."

She bit. "I hate it."

What was really going on? Did Miranda feel responsible for getting Trey to fork over his $3.5 million immediately? We were actually shut down because he hadn't committed, and until he did, the bond company lady wouldn't put her stamp of approval on us for the unions to continue.

The back-and-forth between them continued.

Trey: "I'm mad that you are stressed out."

Miranda: "I really hate it."

Me: "Look, there's a church up there by the side of the road. Let's go pray inside."

We did. The tour bus unloaded all its passengers. Everyone went into the church. I slid into a pew and knelt. I didn't ask about Trey's money. I asked for the tsunami to change its mind and not destroy the East Coast. Then I heard-felt something in my heart: "It must come." I heard-felt the Atlantean reminder: "You must part from your focus on materialism. Balance and change yourselves. Move out of cities into nature. Remember who you really are. You have lost your true identities."

Trey prayed, as did Miranda. I didn't inquire about what they had experienced, nor did I share what I had.

We drove, following behind the bus, to the Caldera. Out of the car and approaching the sunken volcanic crater, I felt as though we'd entered another world. The energy and vibrations slowed down. The silence imploded my ears. There were hardly any animals. A few birds, but not many. The trees and undergrowth were lush. The air actually felt as though it was thinking!

65

We hiked. We could see that a cloud had just lifted out of the crater.

I walked for a while with Trey assisting me. He was sensitive enough to be silent. The ground beneath was unstable and I didn't want to fall. I suggested that Trey and Miranda go on up ahead. I wanted to sit, be silent, and allow. They complied.

There I sat on the side of a hill, feeling into whether I had lived in the area thousands of years ago. My mind fell into pictures.

I saw a small structure that had no interior furniture. There was a mandala on the floor shaped like an exquisite crop circle. I became the shape, which somehow became movement. I felt myself create something to sit on. With my imagination and creativity I fashioned a small couch out of the surrounding tree wood, and when I sat, I could feel that the tree was happy that I appreciated sitting on it. We actually seemed to become one. I couldn't feel any gravity, yet I didn't rise into the air. I just felt that I was suspended into something like time-space. I actually felt that I was living all time and experience at once. At will I could traverse back and forth into what I would define as experiences. And all of them were me. I was different people and they were all me. There were translucent space vehicles outside. They weren't *in* the air, they were *of* the air. *They were propelled by the thoughts of the people inside.* I recognized some of the people. I actually knew them today—in this lifetime. I could feel them think a destination, visualize it, and then dematerialize! Thoughts were not private; everyone was transparent and acknowledged. There were no emotions, only feelings that guided the activities of everyone. The feelings seemed peacefully neutral without any kind of polarity. It was as though everything and everyone simmered at the same temperature. Nothing got cold and nothing boiled over. I *understood* everything around me. My curiosity disappeared. I just *was.*

I'll never forget what happened there. Was that really our state of being at one time? If I was imagining it, why couldn't it be true? Was that why Einstein said imagination was more important than anything else?

Was I in show business because I intuited the importance and the priority of imagination? What else was there? Weren't we all imagining who we were and who and what we wanted to be? Without imagination, there was no life, no civilization, and no movies!

What produces a dream?

Spiritual forces are every bit as real as physical forces if you are attuned to them.

I SLOWLY, gently came back into our three-dimensional reality. I heard the people making their way back up the road toward me. The multi-dimensional reality was over. Then off to the side on a hill above me, I saw a huge human being. He was male and he stood gazing at me. I felt he was real. He was about ten feet tall and I felt he was protective. I stared at him. I could feel his thoughts. He didn't know why I was there. Then he disappeared. He had shown me he was from another time and didn't desire to be in my time any longer. He was proof that all time exists simultaneously.

Trey and Miranda returned with some other tourists, and we traipsed back to the trees and car. We had lunch in a winery owned by the men who ran the tourism trade for the mountain. I sat across from Trey. I had to know whether he would go forward with financing our picture.

"So," I said, "are you in business with Harvey and Bob Weinstein? They've put five hundred thousand dollars into the picture."

"Who?" he said.

"The Weinsteins," I said.

"No," he said. "I know who they are, but supposedly your big investor is Dominick Hollins, who has an island in the Bahamas."

I dropped my fork. "Aren't you Dominick Hollins?"

"Nope," he answered. "Why in the world would you think I was?"

I lost my breath and turned to Miranda, not caring to keep up pretenses any longer. "But you told me he was Dominick Hollins, the big investor," I said in a way that was truly humiliating for everyone involved.

She didn't blink or flinch. "I apologize," she said. "My mistake."

This Trey person was the lover of one of the producers and was a music promoter from L.A. Was life a joke on all of us? Was I set up? Was the UFO story real?

I couldn't swallow lunch, but apparently I could swallow everything else.

Miranda's phone rang. It was Charlie, the transportation coordinator. I waited. Miranda said, "Your agent, Jack, called Charlie to say he's going to call some of his 'friends' in Chicago to come and kill Charlie and Bret. He wants you out of here. He says Charlie needs to book you out on the next plane home."

On the plane back to Gran Canaria, I realized that we had reached the point financially where

I and all the other above-the-line people would need to consider deferring our salaries. That would mean that we would be in fourth position after the movie turned a profit—if that were to happen at all—to get paid a penny. All the other investors would see money first. That wasn't an idea that made me very excited.

ONCE WE got back, Trey pretty much excused himself from my presence until he returned to L.A. But the conversation he had tried to start with me stayed in my head. All my life I have been interested in the possibility of star people having visited the Earth. When I was a kid, I used to gaze up at the stars every night. I *knew* we weren't alone. But I felt alone because I had no one to talk to about it. The first thing I ever asked for was a telescope. And the second thing I asked for was a cross on a chain to wear around my neck. I've never been religious, nor has my family, but as a little girl I somehow felt deeply in a spiritual sense that I needed a cross to go with my telescope. I wore the cross always, and once in Manhattan when I was about eighteen years old, I felt for my cross and it was gone. Right then, a voice came into my head. It said, "Go to Fifty-Seventh and Seventh, to the south-west corner of the street." I walked to that corner and there it was, lying undisturbed on the pavement. I don't know how it got there or when. Ever since then I have learned to listen to what I call "sound guidance"—the little voice in my head that is felt more than heard. We all have one. I felt sound guidance about what to do with our picture. It was faint, but it was there, saying, "Stay."

Anyway, my feeling that there is more life in the universe than what we see on Earth, and that we've been visited by these travelers, has been with me always.

So in my life, my search for the truth is about learning to distinguish between what we are taught and what is actually the truth. They are two entirely different things. I never believed that visitors from the cosmos were a figment of the imagination. I intuited deeply that "they" were observing and sometimes guiding us, if we would be open enough to learn from them.

Acting and show business gave me the opportunity to learn, devise, express, and reflect the truth of human experience. Looking back now, I think I was actually making this movie on this specific location because I desired to learn, devise, express, and reflect the truth of another civilization long ago. I wondered if it would help me understand why we humans were the way we are today. The news every night made it clear we were not on the right path. How did that happen? I've spent a lot of time over the last few years looking for answers to that question. My research became an entertainment, not a particularly pleasant one, but more like science *faction*. And it tied together humanity's reverence for "gods" and events in locations other than Atlantis.

The Dogons are a relatively primitive people living in Mali, formerly a part of French Equatorial Africa. They have preserved over the centuries memories of a tribal connection with Sirius, the Dog Star, which they commemorate with special yearly festivals. Sirius played an important part in the calendar of ancient Egypt relating to the rise and fall of the Nile River. The tribe has long been aware that there is a companion star to Sirius, which we now identify as Sirius B. The Dogons credit their astronomical knowledge to visitors from Sirius and the vicinity, who eons ago brought knowledge of other civilizations and the cosmos to the Earth.

In many places there is prehistoric evidence of visitations by extraterrestrial explorers from close and distant star systems. They brought knowledge of mathematics and cosmic history, the measuring of cosmic time, information about other star systems and about the history of Earth itself long before the Flood, and cultural advances like architectural techniques and record keeping. They brought artifacts that just recently were dated back as far as one million years. They also brought knowledge of cataclysmic geological and weather events on Earth millions of years ago, *before* Atlantis sank.

When I visited and slept in the Great Pyramid of Giza, I asked the custodians there about the still-visible water marks near the base of the pyramid. They claimed the marks were left from the Great Flood, which meant the pyramid was built before the last cataclysm of Atlantis. So, who built the Great Pyramid? The Gods? Again, I asked myself, who were they? And did they, as the Bible said, "Make man in our own image?"

I missed my Terry-Tunes and Buddy-Bubster doggies so much. I longed to cuddle them while falling asleep, not in the least concerned with what had gone on one million years ago in this crazy world.

Because there was no money, our production company cut off the use of the cell phone they had supplied me with. And long-distance calls on the hotel phone were limited to five minutes. I had bought a European cell phone before I left but in all the confusion had canceled it because I thought I wasn't going to leave. I was out of touch, out of comfort, out of love, and slightly out of my mind.

CNN taught me more about Sunni versus Shiite in Iraq. ISIS went on killing people who didn't convert to their idea of God. The German version of *The Sound of Music* set to a Spanish beat leaked over the balconies into my small suite, but it was quieter than before.

Demi Moore arrived and was very sweet. Drank Red Bull all the time and chewed nonsmoking gum. Only ate vegetables and fruit, rubbing her arms and twisting her long brown hair over her shoulder. She was beautiful and nervous and made light, tripping dance moves with her body when she walked. She constantly texted, so when I needed to know where someone was or what was happening with the shooting schedule in light of our nonmoney situation, I asked her.

I wanted to visit Morocco or anywhere, actually, but the bond company said no. I was what they called "the essential" star element for insurance reasons. But since we weren't actually shooting anything at the moment, what exactly was I insurance for?

After a week or two, I was still not over my jet lag. There was something about the vibration in the islands that upset my (and everyone else's) sense of time. It's hard for me to put into words. I often thought of my man-giant Nephilim vision in the Caldera on La Palma. Was I dipping back and forth into the past while struggling with the quantum physics truth that all time is occurring at once and there is no past and no future? There is only now. I wanted to remind our investors of that.

I had dinner with Andy on his birthday and we spoke about the world. He was an avid traveler as I had been. He hadn't attracted coups d'états on his journeys as I had, but he had been around. Once or twice he mentioned the word *deferred* and I expected him to say something about deferring our salaries, but he didn't come out and say it. He professed not to know very much about our film's financial difficulties, but of course he knew every nuance and nook and cranny.

I waited around, ate, and watched CNN. I was fascinated by the abdication of King Juan Carlos and the coronation of his son Felipe as the new King of Spain. The TV reporter described the new monarch as "dignified but relatively austere." Again, I wondered what the world would be like if the Spanish Civil War had not been won by Franco. Would we have avoided suffering through Hitler and the Second World War?

The TV reporter said that Juan Carlos was so emotional during his "decision address" to "his people" that he had to record it several times. I wondered how many takes it had required for a king to get it right? Ah, show business. And his nation's financing was nonexistent too. Over ten percent of his people were unemployed and things were getting worse quickly. Was this the way the world was going? Technology was trumping the employment of actual human beings, and the state of the material world was on its way to disastrous. Was the financial tsunami coming to America too? Who was I kidding? It was already there.

Meanwhile, the Japanese had voted against child pornography but didn't go far enough. You could still buy cartoons of child pornography anywhere, in which two-year-olds were being sexually abused. And they thought that it was normal to be fueling the dark desires of men and criminals that way. A famous cartoonist defended the practice by saying the cartoons were protected by freedom-of-expression laws. Something like the First Amendment in America.

Friends had learned to call me if they wanted to speak to me, because I had no phone to call them. One called and asked if I needed money for food. Another asked if the company had bought a round-trip ticket for me.

I still hadn't heard about the casting of our leading man. Of course not; there was no money to pay him. We couldn't shoot with him anyway. The bond lady waited for our so-called investors to come through. One actor was rumored to have said yes to the part, but when I checked, it turned out his agent refused to let him get on the plane. And his agent was *my* agent—Jack. My tomfoolery was enough for Jack to tolerate. No more of his clients would he put at risk by allowing them to participate in this fiasco! Oh, Hollywood.

I went to see dolphins perform and longed to set them free. How could such majestic creatures live and obey in such soul-cramping spaces? I had read that not only were dolphins equivalent to humans in terms of their intelligence but that their soul memories contained the entire history of humanity on Earth because they had been here that long. The tour buses loaded and unloaded more hordes of expectant tourists everywhere I went.

Nature, the common property of all men, has undergone a transformation.

Regions of the Earth which were formerly inhabited have been destroyed, and former wastelands are full of life.

WE WERE still not shooting. Every now and then the ADs would go out in cars and get traveling location shots that might someday turn out to be necessary.

Andy's back went out. He was up all night every night texting for money to L.A. and various other places. No wonder the loud band didn't bother him! I gave him a bottle of ibuprofen. He said $2 million or so would be coming from a man he knew well. Someone named Dominguen Rays. (Why were all the investors named Dom-something?) Andy said he had been to his home several times and had just talked to him on the phone. Dominguen was coming to the Islands with a million or so to bail us out. I didn't believe it. Andy said he would arrive the next day. Sure . . .

All the actors and Andy had dinner together, making jokes about our situation. Andy said, "If I say anything important, write it down!"

Here are some things I overheard people saying that night:

"I like being anonymous and doing bad things."

"There's nothing like being a belled goat."

"This is the 'have a beer and work on your resume' party."

"*No dinero. No película.*"

"Gin takes you to a place that nothing else takes you to: it sands the edges."

"I have to be daft to work with that man."

"If you can give me a schedule that the bond company approves, I will dance naked upon the sand dunes."

"You need to listen to me more. I am funny."

"Tomorrow night we are going to a gay bar called Das Butt."

"Get off the floor, you'll catch something."

"Fuck the bond company."

"Get your fucking ass out of my face, you asshole."

(The last quote was mine.)

The food was French and excellent, and the wine and fun made for a needed blowout. In front of everyone I bet Andy that Dominguen Rays wouldn't come through with the money. The bet? A week in Paris with no fucking!

Demi and Andy got into a shouting match— something about sexism, I think. I don't know, I left early.

I tried to go to sleep that night by repeating to myself some of the inspirational phrases I had heard over the years:

Let failure be your friend—learn from it.
Look deeply into the appearance of things.
There is brilliance in the Unseen. Feel into it.
Life itself is a profound creative experience.
Become your own creative idea.

I'd try all of the above.

Movies make magic and magic makes movies, but few people realize the grind of detail, blistering hard work, and concentration—even when sleeping—that is required. I'll bet each person working on a movie makes countless lists every day. Here's one of mine:

My List

1. Know my lines.
2. Get up on time.
3. Wear something that works in heat and cold, because the wardrobe department hasn't got enough money for both.
4. Wear walking shoes that can easily be slipped on and off.
5. Wear my mouthpiece splint that aligns my back.
6. Use mouthwash for kissing scenes.
7. Wear socks or stockings so as not to get blisters.
8. Carry paper that has lines big enough to see.

9. Turn off cell phone but have it handy.
10. Carry sugar-free cough drops.
11. Have lots of small bottles of water.
12. Remember to eat, no matter how long a take takes.
13. Check for food between teeth, especially salad.
14. Keep notepaper handy; might want to write a book about all this.
15. Keep head up in the light all day; never mind sleeping.
16. Watch the crew, always.
17. Appreciate and thank them. They are everything.
18. Be nice to director, no matter what.
19. Don't worry whether there is money for next day.
20. Don't worry anyway. It's all happening as it should.

A Second AD's Notes and List

1. Where do we find dressing rooms for the actors? Who will be upset?
2. Are there waiting rooms near where we shoot? Who will be upset?
3. Hire photo doubles and hope the actors don't see them and complain.
4. Hire stunt doubles and don't tell the actors it's necessary.

5. Where is the breakfast for the actors when the call is five a.m.? Some of them can get testy; others are starving themselves anyway—doesn't matter.
6. Faraway locations. What if the actors don't like the hotels? What if they want to drive home to base hotel? What about turnaround time?
7. Have standby drivers in case there's trouble.
8. When should I give the actors their call times? How do I even know? Should I get an international phone for their cell phones? Who will pay?
9. Why am I here?
10. Are we going to shoot a movie . . . or ourselves?

Preparing for a location shoot is a military campaign. The camera crew must take everything necessary for weather, particularly if the director says he wants to shoot in the rain. The director is the dictator on a movie set. There is no such thing as democracy. Directors are often known for their "demanding temperament" and for "being difficult." But there has to be a *decider* about everything—lights, camera, wardrobe, hair, props, speed, emotion, script, pee breaks, crying jags, love affairs, improvisations, ringing cell phones, criticisms, creative differences, and yes, most of all, *acting*. That is the job of the director.

I have never wanted to direct, although I did it once, because I much prefer observing. I love to watch how everyone acts and behaves. Long ago I understood that a film set is akin to a mini civilization populated by artists, carpenters, producers, equipment manufacturers, bankers, clothing stylists, hair stylists, makeup artists, manicurists, caterers, accountants, budget organizers, union representatives, location scouts, studio heads, sanitation workers, seamstresses, travel agents, police, and schoolteachers (for young actors).

When you live and breathe a film set, as I have for so long, you become a political activist. How can everyone get along while attempting to accomplish a human drama-dream? I never wanted to be president-dictator-decider. As Chauncey Gardiner said in *Being There*, "I like to watch."

So the company moved to shoot in Las Palmas.

The magic of what we were doing hit me when I walked into the actual church that Christopher Columbus prayed in the night before he commenced his voyage west. I wondered, How could a building sustain itself for such a long period of time, through so much history? Not knowing about the New World, Columbus called the inhabitants that he encountered when he made landfall Indians, because he thought he had landed in India. I stood before the altar of the ancient church and thought how appropriate it was, even if he didn't realize it, that he left for the New World from the last remaining remnants of the Old World of Atlantis.

The Catholic Church is certainly the longest-running governing body of the modern world. I wondered what kind of religion they'd practiced in Atlantis. Did the Pleiadian and Arcturian star visitors want to be seen and known as gods? Did they regard us as their children? How could we honestly rely on the truth of the existence of anything that existed 870,000 years ago and then disappeared? It was soul-searing to imagine all that being snuffed out. But then, many people today constantly speak of our own End Times.

Back on the set, Billy Connolly's character was to usher me around and impress me as he played his con-man tricks. We shot at authentic museums that housed treasured replicas of the *Niña*, *Pinta*, and the *Santa Maria*. How could those sailors have tolerated such a long and terrifying journey on what we would deem a medium-sized sailboat?

Because of the moderate trade winds, sailors from Europe preferred to set out on their voyages from the Canary Islands. The technological advances and creative flowering of the Renaissance period contributed to the discovery of new routes. So Columbus's leaving for the New World from the Canary Islands was not a random choice. The archipelago of the Islands occupies a position that facilitates navigation toward the west owing to its trade winds and sea streams. That was why all expeditions would stock up on supplies here before crossing the Atlantic. During this period a real social, cultural, and economic exchange linked the New World with Europe. The Islands became a trading market and a fountainhead for immigration. They were called "a nation maker" because of the immigrants they sent to the Americas.

One of the first products to come from the Canary Islands that became an industry in the Americas was sugar. The people from the Islands brought sugar to America, as well as their families. Sometimes I wish they'd left the sugar behind.

Sugar was one of the items that shaped the culture of the Americas. Since the Canaries were part of the shipping route for sugarcane as well as a center of its cultivation and refining, they enacted trade policies that led to a commercial boom for the economy of the Islands and the Flemish sugar plantation owners, agents, and traders. Sugar was one of the principal motors for the economies of Spain, Holland, and the Americas.

Under the protection of the sugarcane business came Flemish art, which was dedicated to ornamenting and improving the sugarcane ranches and the chapels and convents. It was a way of affirming the personality and social prestige of the new sugar population. It became the "Atlantic sugar culture." And America became the New World and a vast new market that was addicted to the substance that was most damaging to our mind, body, and spirit, to say nothing of our teeth.

I had been in the Canaries since June 6. It was now June 21. We had shot intermittently and made jokes about leaving. I was relatively happy with simply observing what was going on. I was detached while flowing with the go, shopping with Miranda, and reminding myself that the whole experience would make a good script or book. I wasn't the only one. Others were making notes, laughing and crying as they scribbled.

On June 21 I got a call from a friend in the States. He said he had talked to someone he knew whom Miranda had recently called. During this phone call, according to my friend's friend, she'd complained that I was a bitch, a "loco gringita," as she put it. I was told she had also placed pictures of me and comments on Facebook and promised there would be many more. She said she was going to write a book about me. My friend said, "Don't trust her. She's telling people you are a tyrant and very demanding. I don't know what her game is."

I didn't either. It certainly wasn't people-pleasing for money, and I knew I didn't match her description of me. It truly unsettled me. Miranda was the person I hung out with the most and depended upon. I thought we had a good relationship.

I asked her to take down the Facebook stuff but said nothing else. My mind raced. Why would she do such a thing? I knew she wanted to be a Hollywood producer, but did she think this was the avenue to that end?

After a few days of not knowing what to do, I confronted her and the producer she worked for. He was confounded and, if my friend was right, Miranda deserved an Oscar for her denial. In fact, I almost believed her. What did she want? Why was she doing this?

I thought maybe she had two personalities or something. Then I overheard her making reservations at a restaurant that was overbooked. She said (while crying) that her husband was dying and we needed to have a family reunion for comfort. It worked: we got seated.

My friend said I should call Interpol and have myself rescued from Miranda. Instead, at least for the time being, I found her manipulation of truth fascinating and entertaining to watch. But I knew I'd have to keep a close watch so that it didn't lead to more serious trouble.

The fourth dimension
is defined as an *idea*.
Where is it? Anywhere.
Where did it come from?
Nobody knows.
Where will it end?
Impossible to say.
It is without a beginning
and without an end.

AS WE waited for Dominguen Rays to make good on his promise to Andy and send money, I had lots of things to keep my mind occupied.

1. Jessica was coming back from her time off. Why?

2. There was a monstrous forest fire not far from my house in Santa Fe. Did I need to get home and do something?

3. I heard more of the gossip that Miranda was telling her friends in the States. Evidently, she would get drunk on champagne, then complain endlessly about me and her boss, one of our producers. But mostly she'd go on about how much she wanted to get laid.

4. Who doesn't?

5. One afternoon, I came upon Tyne sobbing in the lobby. "Everyone treats me like trash," she wailed. I felt sorry for her. Lying was one thing, and probably was sometimes a job requirement for producers. But amateur night? Yes, that can be destructive too. I told

her that if our picture ever got made and became a success, she'd better get prepared to produce another one. I continued, "You aren't prepared, even though it says 'producer' by your name." I knew her lying in the line of duty wouldn't stop. I wondered what would be next. I found out soon enough.

6. I decided to walk to the nude beach. I didn't walk oceanside because there were rocks and too many people. I was deciding as I walked whether I wanted to see the plain straight nude beach or the gay nude beach. After hiking nearly an hour in the heat and still not getting to either one, I turned back. But I got reports. Many single men, gay or straight, faced the ocean and stretched in the sun, standing up to prove to their neighbors that they were proud to be there. Straight couples for the most part just lay in the sun, while the gay crowd was more active, gossiping, joking, flirting, and swimming together in the sea.

7. I was beginning to feel really cynical when ICM (my talent agency) informed me that legally it was all right for me to stay here and wait for the money if I was that stupid. All independent films were having similar money problems. The independent movie business and the studios had both been taken over by corporations and wannabes.

Our purpose on Earth today is to manifest the divine and the beautiful.

The alternative is to experience miserable failure again.

ONE MORNING I was having breakfast in the room set aside for cast members when I heard Tyne scream. She was staring at her laptop. She stood up with the computer and showed me an email from Dominguen Rays. "This is a definite commitment of money," she said. "Look, he signed it and he's committing one-point-five million to me."

I looked at it. I wasn't a producer or money person (obviously) but it looked okay to me. "Are emails legal commitments?" I asked.

"Yes," she answered. "It's a commitment by email. And he can be sued."

Andy had said it was definite, and according to the email exchange with Rays, the money was coming. Something didn't sit right with me, yet how could this guy make such blatant statements of commitment and not be good for it? I thought of something I'd heard from a businessman friend of mine: "Form a corporation, promise money, default, and declare bankruptcy in that corporation . . ." A corporation couldn't be sued if it was bankrupt. Or something like that.

Miranda looked up and ordered an iced coffee

from the roaming busboy. "Did you see?" she said, gesturing to the departing busboy. "How he loves looking at my face, particularly when I ask him for something? Everyone here loves me when I put my hands up around my face. Especially when I say 'burger.' I'll have a burger."

I gulped. What planet was I on? People are always fascinating if you really look at them.

Extravagant use of self brings on destructive forces.

BACK IN the first few days of shooting, we still didn't have a leading man (the part Alan Arkin was supposed to play). Now, the leading man was supposed to work the following morning and I finally found out who had been cast.

Howard Hesseman lived in Paris with his wife and was enjoying his life. He had planned to go to the South of France the next morning when he got a call from our production offering him the part and asking him to come to the Canary Islands instead. He said yes and got on the late plane. No one from our company had met him, but I soon learned he was adorable, funny, crazy, and so talented he would have made Alan Arkin flinch.

We actually shot the scene! We became friends. A few nights later, several of us had dinner to celebrate the feast of San Juan, which meant we had to secretly write down on a scrap of paper the things we desired to be rid of for the next year. We were then to burn them in a fire on the beach. We chose to make a fire in the fountain| of the hotel.

My piece of paper had two words: *Wild Oats*.

I turned on the news again. My favorite comedy-relief entertainment was always there with something different to show me. But these days, what they were broadcasting seemed to have turned from a comedy show to horror. The world appeared to be falling apart and the celebration of hate and violence was the new theatrical art form. It wasn't just the theater of ISIS's brand of violent art. It was Putin playing sly dictator, the robbing of the people aboard the downed Malaysian airline, natural disasters where the Earth seemed to be shaking off the nuisance of its human presence, people stealing tombstones from cemeteries and selling them and other graveyard artifacts. Selling tombstones and personal possessions from dead people was a kind of materialism beyond my imagination.

What was happening to our human stage play? We were participating willingly in a theatrical extravaganza of the End Times. What would Shakespeare have had to say about this life being a stage and all of us actors strutting our will upon it?

Even the news spoke of the various "theaters of war" and who the "actors" were in the game of life and death and global conquest. Was everyone alive starring in his or her own movie and basically looking for new sources of financing? So many people spent the majority of their lives in pursuit of either money or God. Had money actually become our common God?

It occurred to me that what was going on in show business was a pretty good analogy to what was destroying the human race. Our studio system had been taken over by corporate thinking, reducing the art form of film to the *branding* of everything dear to human expression. Our civilization itself was becoming subservient to whatever the corporate global elite decided was important to them. They valued money exchange, political exchange, religious exchange, and they even designed the exercises of war and killing.

The corporate studio elite in Hollywood knew that violent action films about war and horror and death made more money than anything else, even if the wars happened to be conducted on another planet in another universe. Make another group into an enemy, and yours will have to beat them to survive. The secret to the success of the powerful few seemed to be their skillful use of the Malthusian theories of divide and conquer. Doing whatever it took to create divisions in a society became the new global art form— divisions within communities, within religions, within races, within the sexes, and even within nature. Divide—divide—divide with power and money.

I failed to understand, though. What did the corporate power brokers get out of doing all this? More money, more power? Why? They didn't have the time to enjoy what they already had. They spent their lives in a never-ending circle of repetitive, violent competition.

So bowing down to the wishes and desires of the corporate elite in the studios and on the world stage was the creed by which we were all expected to live. What happened to individual expression? It had been reduced to carefully monitored protests on the streets, in governments, and even within families.

The art form of humanity expressing life on the screen had fallen victim to the same powerful influences. In the old days in Greece, audiences used to go to the theater to experience their "godhead" potential. They went for inspiration, joy, laughs, dramatic solutions, and a thrilling recognition of their own humanity in the events they saw taking place on the stage. Nowadays, who is there for us to identify with? Characters in *Spiderman 13*, or *Expendables 4*, or *Adventures of Super Hero #20*?

The corporate thinkers would much rather cater to lowest-common-denominator humanity because doing so makes money. Anything to keep the people from thinking is their approach. The corporate thinkers of the television networks are just as guilty. In fact, they *are* the corporate elite because they control information. We are not seeing the truth on our news shows. We are seeing the *designed* truth. I fail to see the purpose of designed truth. Underneath, we all know what is true. Therefore, we are becoming a human culture of suspicious skeptics. It is easier to control a skeptical public because you can manipulate them more easily with fear.

I guess it's also possible that someone who is imbued with and educated in the manipulations of show business has a more honest bead on what's happening in the world than, say, the CIA, governments, bankers, and news organizations because they know how to *charge* the public for designed truth. Therefore, that makes us all guilty . . .

Perhaps we should defer our lives, not just our salaries.

All of life should have a new concept
of a divine government.

DEFERRING OUR salaries is, of course, what came up next. The word came that Dominguen Rays was indeed full of crap. "The commitment was not real," said Tyne. *No shit.* "The money didn't come through." *Oh, really?*

I asked what the lawyer for the crew was recommending. The answer: *"Strike!"* I said, "If they go, I go. I'm a liberal!" A bleeding-heart liberal is what my father called me. But then he voted for Nixon, happily.

There was a conference call with the bond lady scheduled to decide what to do.

I had a long talk with Demi and Jessica. Demi said Andy had texted her that the Rays money was coming. Was he lying? I asked Miranda. She said, "Well, some money came in. Maybe that's what he meant." Did she know more than she was saying? She ordered a burger and said, "Don't you love how he [the waiter] loves to see my face say 'burger'?" *Jesus. Is this what you call amateur diversionary tactic? Fascinating.*

I called Jack. "What should I do?" All my team back home said, "Wait until Wednesday, the day the bond company makes a decision."

"Should I defer my salary?" I asked Jack.

He was swift. "Defer what? There's no money to defer. What would they reward you with—their firstborn?" I laughed. Hard. Then, well, show business is show business!

I wondered what Miranda was reporting to her friends back home.

I noticed a change in attitude toward me from production personnel. It was obvious they were being extra nice . . . too nice . . . too sweet, especially Andy. That's when I knew there would be a meeting about deferring pay and production basically depended on me.

Jack called and said he couldn't get anyone to talk to him. I said, "Send the guys from Chicago, they'll get some action." Jack then sent a directive to production that he wanted me on a plane out of there by Friday.

I told Jessica. She said, "If you go, I go. I'll call my agent." Jessica's agent was on vacation. Smart guy.

The jokes about shutting down got funnier and more preposterous, and then they began to seem seriously real.

We can hear every quiver
of the air if we listen.

SHOW BUSINESS people, for the most part, will be with you to the end. Except for a few divas and strutting manager-agent types, show business people on the front lines stick together until the project is completed. It's in our DNA to guarantee that the show *will* go on. Most other businesses are more left-brained and know when to quit. They don't throw good money after bad, nor do they waste their time and intelligence on something they think won't make any money. Not so with show people. I really don't know why. Perhaps it is the ever-hopeful, game-playing child in all of us. Whatever the circumstances, we plow ahead because it's our chance to be seen and acknowledged. Are we the prime example of human beings' need to be loved? Do we (crew included) work to make magic because of something in our human nature? Are we the same people engaged in the same play since childhood, the ones who didn't ever want to come inside and wash up and sit down to dinner? No, we'd rather keep playing, even if it means missing out on dinner. We'd rather play than eat; we'd rather play than work; we'd rather play than sleep; we'd rather play than learn lessons. In fact, learning about ourselves *was* the lesson. Nothing else could come close to educating us about the magic of which we were all capable. We'd even rather play than make money! The producers and agents don't understand what personal magic there is in playing. We actor/director/writer people make up our own play in order to reflect life itself back to ourselves. For me, would the decision to defer my salary in order to keep shooting be about playing the role of someone who loved to play? Or would it be just plain stupid to walk away?

There was much talk about how our business had changed since the corporate takeover of the studios. We all knew the good movies that said something about the human condition were the independently produced movies. The grind of creativity was what we enjoyed and were rewarded by.

We did scenes in the blinding sun and heat, over and over. We were diligent in our striving for perfection. We worked sixteen hours a day. We were nice to people we couldn't bear. We were the definitions of cooperation and collaboration. Want specifics? Our perspiration ruined our makeup, and there was no end to the torture of an itching wig kept in place by hairpins that dug into our sweating scalps day after day. To use our own hair under these conditions would have been ridiculous. With the heat and perspiration, the real hair wouldn't match. It would be curly on take one, but totally straight by take seven. The sweat soaked through our clothes, making odd designs under our arms and across our chests.

An actor who was supposed to appear in one of our scenes was also an investor (a very small one). But he missed the plane in Madrid, so he was not present for his two lines. Oddly, his money didn't materialize either.

We looked forward to the evening drink on the big patio *before* the band began.

Andy called for Jessica, Demi, and me to join him on the patio. He outlined what the money situation was. He was open and specific. He told us that he was going to defer and asked if we would too. He said, "The footage is wonderful. Jessica is funnier than she thinks she is, and you, Shirley, are a machine."

What does that mean? I wondered. Was I a machine because I was always on time, knew my lines, and could act? Did that make me a machine? I understood that my work ethic was reliable, but how was my performance? I just knew José Luis was photographing me to look forty and I was worried. The roles for me now were definitely older women. That's where the work was. I actually hoped I didn't look too good.

Jessica and Demi and I carried on the conversation when Andy left us. About ten of the below-the-line people (crew, production, etc.) had deferred part of their salaries. Now was the time for above-the-line (actors, directors, writers) to step up to the plate.

Jessica and Demi said, "Let's call our manager." (They had the same one.) I didn't have a manager. I had an agent who knew the business better than anyone and was going to order a Sicilian hit on whomever he could round up. He had specifically said to me, "Do not defer before talking to me." Now he couldn't get anyone on the phone. Production people didn't just fall off the turnip truck either. That's why they didn't accept his calls.

There had been divisive scenes in the production office. The Americans couldn't get along or understand the Spanish way of working. The Spanish felt that Nick, the AD, yelled too much at the crew. But we all knew that an AD has to be a mixture of Hitler and Gandhi. The Spanish had a different sense of time—more laissez-faire, more concerned with manners and politeness. The American way of working was get the job done in as little time as possible because time is money.

There had also been arguments as to who was in charge of what. I saw in action how matriarchal the Spanish pecking order was. The men might be macho strutters, but it was the women in charge of an aspect of production who snapped the decision-making whip. A woman headed up the Spanish production company, which provided all the equipment, cameras, and gear, and everything else that the below-the-line crew needed. Appar-ently, she had also put four hundred thousand toward the budget. The American way of working would have to defer to the Spanish way. I laughed to myself. Deferment seemed to be something the Americans were going to have to get used to in order to get the movie made.

Jessica and Demi's manager didn't spend much time on the phone with them. "If that's what you want to do, go for it," he said. They were willing. So now it was up to me. What bothered me, even in my state of liberal, bleeding-heart flexibility, was that we would be the last to get paid, after all the other investors were paid off (assuming the picture made any money at all). We three would actually be investors, but with a third or fourth position of recoupment. That could really mean we would have worked for nothing, or close to it. Was that fair?

I told Jessica and Demi that I thought we should defer half our salaries, but I wanted to get a specific recommendation from my agent. And my agent wasn't on vacation. So we broke up the meeting and scattered before the horrible band started their first set.

Andy joined me in my room. We called Jack. For once in his life, he wasn't in! Andy told me that Michelos would be out about a million dollars if the film fell apart. I knew that Michelos had been stalwart with his money and support. He had also been one of the producers of *Elsa & Fred*, a movie I'd made with Christopher Plummer. Jack told me Michelos hadn't really put any of his own money in either production. I didn't know who to believe. I only knew Michelos had lost twenty-five pounds and seemed quietly hysterical. Every time I saw him in the lobby, he would run up to me and say, "Everything will be fine. I know it," and in his charming way try to reassure me. He did, however, change his stripes when he spoke about Tyne. "I'm going to kill her," he'd say. "This is all her fault." I thought of getting a few of Jack's Sicilians sent over to us so each could blame the other if Tyne bit the dust. Michelos said, "The deal for investors that Tyne has arranged is so convoluted that investors don't want to risk coming in. In other words, this film has bad juju for investors."

So Michelos hated Tyne, Jack hated Michelos, the Spanish crew hated the American AD, the American production office hated the Spanish production office . . . Thank God everybody loved the caipirinhas!

The male actors seemed to be removed from

all of this drama. I don't think they felt the same level of involvement with the picture, and that wasn't their fault. No one from production ever met them in Madrid to respectfully welcome them to the movie. (One actor hadn't even been told which hotel to go to, so he nearly turned around to go back home.) That meant that an American production coordinator hadn't done his job. When confronted with this fact, he said, "I thought the Spanish were supposed to take care of that." I watched all this and noticed that the American spent most of his time surfing the Internet and gossiping. The Spanish noticed it too. So, more bad blood.

Was this the sort of thing that caused Atlantis to sink? I began to see little difference between what was happening on CNN news and what was going on with the film, except for the killing part. And it was going to get worse.

Man, in times of distress,
has always called on God,
the Great Spirit, the Creator.

The Atlanteans were divided into two distinct classes: the Sons of the Night and Sons of the Sun.

Ancient books tell us of terrible clashes between the two.

JACK CALLED back. I explained what Andy had outlined and his concern for Michelos. Jack screamed, "Michelos owes another client of mine fifty thousand dollars! He's full of shit!" Then I was treated to one of Jack's irresistible, impressive, curse-filled screaming rants, all based on his love for me, which finally ended with the words *"And they are disrespecting you!"*

This was the classic Italian, family-centric point of view. I really didn't give a damn how they were treating me. That was up to me anyway. But Jack was an old-school, brilliant-but-not-diplomatic, totally-involved-with-his-clients, rare, and respected agent. I tried to calm him down. No luck. I could see why the production office wouldn't take his calls anymore. But he was right when he asked the big question: "What are the terms of your deferment?"

Demi and Jessica texted Andy the news that they would defer. Okay. Now *I* was in an untenable position. Everyone had deferred but me. I had no choice. I had to defer *now* or we didn't work tomorrow. I couldn't wait for Jack to work out the terms of my deferment.

I asked Andy, "Who owns this film?" He said, "Let me put it this way. José Luis and I have the only hard copy of what we've already shot."

I frankly didn't know what that meant, or would ever mean, in a show business court of law. I called Michelos and said, "Okay, I'll defer without knowing the exact terms, but you promise me that you'll finance or get the financing for the picture I want to do next."

He promised. I could hear Jack laughing.

I informed everyone I would defer, now draw up the paperwork. A few days later I signed the papers, only to be told they had made some mistakes and I needed to sign the corrected ones in a few days. My question: Are we working or not? Yes, we were ready to work.

I was sick and tired of trying to keep up with amateur hour. The bond company still hadn't signed off on us. The actor who had missed his plane in Madrid reported us to the Screen Actors Guild, which meant we were now truly in jeopardy of shutting down. However, when SAG got word that Jessica, Demi, and I would defer, they gave us a little more time.

We continued shooting. We worked sixteen-hour days and shot in whatever weather was available. It didn't matter that our working conditions were confusing and sometimes intolerable. I could feel everyone watching me. At my age, would I continue? It never occurred to me not to, and I never needed a wheelchair or a doctor or a nap. At the root of who I was professionally, I knew I was still a dancer. And dancers go on regardless and don't complain. I remembered, at the age of seventeen, falling during the warm-up for a ballet I was doing at Constitution Hall in Washington, D.C. I sprained my ankle badly, didn't tell anyone, and danced on point until I collapsed after curtain calls. If I could get through that, anything else was possible.

During the shoot, which I was now actually enjoying, Billy Connolly and Howard Hesseman were so adorably funny that I sometimes laughed so hard we had to cut so I could recover. I don't think it was gallows humor because of our financial circumstances. It was these guys. They were hilarious but in the most wonderfully subtle way—real experts—so exquisitely tuned to comedic delivery. The two of them were brilliant on or off the set. Long conversations with them about the events of their lives made our picture-making a holiday. During one sequence we shot (or tried to shoot), I broke up and was recorded laughing for seven minutes straight! I only hoped the audience would find it all as funny as I did.

I thought a lot about what provokes laughter. Why do some people find something funny and others don't? I realized that my laughter was based more and more on cynicism as I got older.

I often found humor in the efforts of some people to appear one way when they were so clearly the opposite. But that wasn't the case with my costars. When Howard described how terrified he was of *not* being funny, he was hilarious. When Billy recounted the horror of his childhood, I was on the floor. And when we all compared notes about what scared us the most, we would have made Charlie Chaplin proud.

I've always subscribed to the saying "Death is easy, comedy is hard." Perhaps you couldn't have one without the other. I've heard more funny lines said at funerals than anywhere else. Comedy rests on contradictions. For example, if a beggar walks down the street and falls into a manhole, that's not funny. But if an elegantly dressed, powerful, rich, upper-crust man falls into a manhole, that's funny. The contradiction of pretense, manners, and behavior makes comedy work. That was the genius of Chaplin and, for example, Mel Brooks's "Springtime for Hitler." Or even of Rob Ford, the mayor of Toronto. Contradictions make comedy funny—and make life interesting. I guess that means we have to have the polarity of tragedy and comedy to make life work.

All the while, as I worked and laughed and thought, I was always aware in the back of my consciousness that we were probably having our adventure on the remnants of Atlantis. The air, the sense of time, the frequent imbalance of the land itself made the place different from anywhere else I had ever been. The behavior of the personnel on the movie was more direct and honest when their emotions were activated. People described experiencing a kind of "cleansing" feeling. I wondered out loud whether we were "cleansing our karma," so to speak. Was that the reason we were making the movie here? Even the hordes of German tourists figured into the mix of Atlantis, but I couldn't understand why. Were we experiencing our own sinking and turmoil in order to work out our personal, unresolved issues?

I began to look for where I could find more material on Atlantis—myths, history, dreams, fiction, esoteric writings. I had been exposed to channeling for many years. Channeling is when someone with special abilities is able to receive information directly from a spiritual entity. In my experience, some of the information that comes through is accurate—some not.

In between setups I researched any information I could find on the legend of Atlantis. The why of its downfall, whether you believe it's a myth or real, seemed analogous to what I was seeing in the world today. There have been several golden ages in our human experience, but none seemed to have achieved the sophisticated spiritual level of Atlantis. Was that because advanced star beings were part of, or maybe even rulers of, such a successful civilization? Had those star beings learned from their own cosmic dramas, and were they familiar with the heartbreaking results of unchecked power, materialism, and manipulation of fear and division? Was all life in the universe saddled with the same polarities as we were experiencing?

I was pondering some of these thoughts one day as we waited in the hot sun for Jessica to get ready for the shot. I usually can feel when something is taking longer than it should. Every actress in the world takes longer than me because I just walk away from the mirror and devise ways to finish the makeup and hair process while I'm walking. It's really not fair to the artists of makeup and hair, but that's the way I work. Anyway, Jessica had a wardrobe and makeup and hair change which seemed to be taking longer than it should. Just as I was about to ask the AD what was going on, she appeared. She was clearly distraught as she explained, "I hate to keep people waiting. Please understand that nobody knocked on my door to call me. I've been in my dressing room waiting for an hour!"

I can't tell you how many times that has happened to me and to others that I've worked with. Many times Elizabeth Taylor was accused of keeping people waiting on the set, when she never heard the call. Why we don't hear the call is a mystery. The assistant directors (ADs) are sometimes afraid to disturb a star even though time means everything and *they* know that *we* know that. Is it out of too much respect for privacy? Or maybe an AD doesn't like the star and this is a good way to make a point. Or maybe they do call us and we don't want to hear it. We need more time but don't want to ask for it. We happen to be doing something else important. We fall asleep waiting and don't hear it. We don't like the script or the director or anyone else, for that matter. It's a way of asserting a little bit of personal power. So many possibilities.

I don't have any idea what happened with Jessica that particular day. What concerned me was what effect the disruption would have on Jessica's performance. We had a dramatic scene to play in the hot sun, a scene in which she was supposed to cry. We absolutely had to get the scene within the hour or we would fall behind and there was no money to cover a reshoot.

Jessica pulled herself together. Andy yelled, "Action." Without a moment to prepare and with a jittery crew looking on, Jessica was brilliant in the scene and cried exactly on cue. I couldn't believe it.

"Cut!"

I said, "Jessica, you are good, good, good. How did you do that?"

"I guess I have a well of sorrow in my life," she answered with a little smile.

I thought of Misha Baryshnikov and Sam Shepard, but I didn't ask one single question. I knew I was in the presence of a great actor.

The crew was upset, and I heard that Katey, the second AD who was supposed to call Jessica, had quit. Nick would have to get someone else quickly. Without good ADs a picture can truly fall apart.

I turned to Andy to ask what had happened. He just shrugged. "It doesn't matter as long as the scene works . . ." That's show business.

Morale among the Spanish crew was low. They had little knowledge of set organization, their rhythm of life was different from ours, and they basically weren't getting paid. I appreciated that they would work at all. They knew that I and everyone else above the line had deferred. The love of show business prevailed. We worked because of and for each other.

I hounded Katey to come back, or at least to meet me for a drink and talk. She finally agreed to a meeting. She said she had been unhappy with the conditions on the set for a while. When she was hired, apparently Tyne never mentioned to her that she wouldn't be paid the base second AD salary. Katey overlooked that, however, because she loved the idea of shooting on the

Canary Islands, and she loved the script and the cast. But basically she wanted to become a producer and handle artistic problems and questions, not production problems. I understood her feelings but warned her that quitting this job would not be good for her reputation. She understood but decided to leave anyway. I liked her a lot—for her honesty, her organizational skills, and her personality. All three would allow her to over-come any repercussions her departure from *Wild Oats* might bring about. However, she and I both knew there would be even more complicated communication problems between the Spanish and American crews in the days ahead, and she didn't feel the need to be in the middle of all that.

As I watched and experienced other acts of cultural noncommunication, I felt more and more that the underlying cause of most conflict was money. Even on a set where people were primarily motivated by their love of making movies, money was a culprit. Was there any endeavor on the planet that could be thoroughly enjoyed without being tainted by questions of financial compensation?

It was a long day and a longer night as I spoke to friends in California who gave me new evidence that the radiation from the Fukushima nuclear reactor meltdown in Japan had reached the west coast of the United States and was soaking into their skin every moment! I heard that Miranda had referred to me as a dodo bird to someone. That's when I fell asleep.

The next day we did a funny scene. Again I laughed so hard at Billy and Howard that I had stomach pains. Another actor reported our non-payments to SAG. They said they'd give us three more days or they'd shut us down. The paper-work for the deferments hadn't yet gone through.

The man in charge of transportation dreamt that Jack shot him in the heart. Bret, the unit production manager, said the guys from Sicily were on their way.

We started shooting at eight a.m. and finished at midnight. Whoever was there to gun down anybody would have to do it under the lights and in front of the camera. At the end of the shoot, I was so tired I was afraid I would fall. Countless arms were offered to help me. Despite all the mayhem, I felt secure.

Some of the crew thought Andy was a bull. I agreed—an artistic bull—and that's exactly what we needed. He knew what he wanted, and he had a concise rhythm with his comedy. Our money debacle never seemed to bother him. If he needed more takes, he asked for them regardless of what that entailed (money, energy, or time). Good for him.

Since my makeup artist was married to José

Luis, the director of photography, I was privileged to hear a great deal of inside information. We were to shoot in New Orleans in a month and neither she nor José Luis had been told if they were going. It would be a disaster if they didn't. We would inevitably look like different people on-screen. When I inquired, I made it clear to the production office that I considered their presence essential to my ability to continue filming. I was pretty sure José and Mariló would be joining us in New Orleans!

Miranda suddenly became very sweet and seemingly dedicated to ensuring my well-being. What was going on?

One of the scenes that was most important to Andy, whether we had the money or not, took place on an airplane. It was the transition scene as the two women departed for their adventure. He had written it to take place on seats that reclined all the way back. Iberia said they didn't have any seats like that. Andy said he had flown on an Iberian plane *with* seats like that. There was much to-and-froing about which airliner had what, and he found what he wanted on an Iberian jetliner parked somewhere in a hangar in an airport in Madrid.

The company moved to Madrid.

I had begun to realize how deeply my meta-physical and spiritual search had been connected to Spain. I had been to Madrid several times before, but what registered with me more than anything was that I'd begun and finished my life-changing experience walking the medieval pilgrimage of the Santiago de Compostela (also called the Camino, which means "the Way") in Madrid. Then I had a backpack and a bottle of water with me. Now I had an entire film crew. I had had many past-life recalls on the Camino, so many that at times it seemed as though I was watching a movie in my own head—a movie of my past lives that allowed me to discover how they karmically played out with one another.

On the Camino, I'd remembered a lifetime I had as a Moroccan girl in the Middle Ages. In that life I'd always worn a Celtic cross around my neck as protection against Christians, Arabs, and other rival tribes of the time. In my present life, as I'd trekked through a village, I'd walked past a small jewelry store in whose front window a Celtic cross was displayed. I recognized it and went in to ask about it. The proprietor said it had once belonged to a Moroccan girl who wore it as protection from the tribes of the time! I bought it, put it on, and it has never left me since that day. Of course I had the cross with me on location in Madrid. Wherever I go, I always sleep with it beside my bed. Whenever I look at it, I'm reminded that my life itself seems to be a Camino, a long journey full of unexpected discoveries about myself and the people and places around me. The Way is both a journey and a destination.

At the end of the Camino de Compostela, I came to the town of Finisterre. When I asked what the word *finisterre* meant, I was told, "the end of the known world." Did that suggest that there had been another world further to the west in the Atlantic Ocean? In my private conversations with Spaniards, the subject then and now always seemed to come around to a place called Atlantis. People seemed to intuit it as a "real myth," a shadow of a past they understood almost mystically. In Spain, the people recognized an "underneath truth" they seemed to want to remember and touch.

In my research, I came across an Atlantean ritual that involved huge bulls. The animals were both revered and feared. They were sacred and were used in dangerous ritual ceremonies in which teams of young male and female contestants competed in vaulting over the bull's back through his sharp horns. This ritual competition may have been the basis for the Greek legend of the sacrifice of youths to the Minotaur—a monstrous half-human bull.

In Charles Berlitz's book *Atlantis: The Eighth Continent*, he describes another tradition of Atlantis this way: "When the ten hereditary kings of Atlantis met in council on public affairs alternately every five and six years, they first performed sacrifices in what was a sort of royal bullfight." This ritual involved bulls that had the range and freedom to roam the temple of Poseidon, where the ten kings were left alone with them. After the kings offered prayers to the gods that they might find the sacrifices acceptable to them, they hunted the bulls armed only with staves and nooses. The bull they caught was led up to a sacred column, struck on the head, and slain over the sacred inscription of the Laws of Atlantis. These laws were inscribed on a pillar made of the mysterious metal orichalcum. Next to the laws, there was inscribed an oath invoking mighty curses on the disobedient.

Royal bulls, Minotaurs, ritualistic sacrifice of the sacred animal done with respect and ceremony —and after Atlantis, bull worship and sacrifice—spread across the ancient world: Crete, Egypt, North Africa, Iberia, and a number of Latin and South American countries.

Were these traditions a whisper of proof that we were the inheritors of the misty beginnings of prehistory in Atlantis?

I wondered, Who were the ten kings, and who were the gods they worshipped?

In Genesis 6:4, we are told, "There were giants in the Earth in those days; and also after that when the sons of God came in unto the daughters of men and they bore children to them, the same became mighty men which were of old, men of renown."

There are so many references in ancient texts to gods from heaven mating with humans and producing offspring, from texts that predate the Bible, which itself says, "We will make man in our own image." There are many plural references to gods—not God.

My mind swirled as I devoured the research. There were organized cultures seventy-five thousand years before the present time. The theory of civilizations rising and declining like great moving wheels was succinctly expressed by Greek historians, not just Plato, who suggested that civilizations meet cataclysmic ends approximately once every ten thousand years.

I read that an ancient artifact, a silver chalice of intricate design, was discovered embedded in a granite rock split in Dorchester, Massachusetts. The time needed to have the rock form around it suggested that the chalice possessed an age of hundreds of thousands of years or, more likely, over a million years!

I thought of my past-time recollections as I walked the Camino to Finisterre. Was I remembering my past lives, or was I simply living them at the same time as I was living this one? Stephen Hawking once told me, "There never was a beginning and there will never be an end. It is all now."

There I was, an actress on location in what could have been the remnants of Atlantis, doing scene after scene with no money or material reward. What was the difference between understanding that all experience is occurring simultaneously and playing a scene where I believed I was actually the person I was playing, yet simultaneously knew I was really still myself? Both were real. Both occupied my consciousness at the same time. It was all happening *now* and I felt comfortable in understanding that that must be true for life itself. We are all busily playing our parts while sensing that we are many people at the same time. Life is show business. The Bard was the real scientist.

I might be concerned that there wasn't enough money to shoot our current "play." But maybe that was our saving grace. To go on creating something we believed in, regardless of the material gain attached to it, was to engage in work of a higher order. I gathered that made our undertaking quite unlike what had happened in Atlantis. The great civilization seemed to have collapsed from giving spiritual priority to greed, power, materialism, and acquisition. I wondered, Were men in charge back then too? Wasn't the authentic human soul always intended to be androgynous?

EVER SINCE I was a kid old enough to have real thoughts that I could remember, I've wondered what the soul was. How was it different from the mind? Was our soul our real identity?

In my thirties, I went into a long series of meditations looking for some answers. I went far back into time, almost before there was form, before we had bodies, before life became what we think of as "alive."

Something like a light was embodied in a soft, bubbling matter. So long as the soft, bubbling matter had not become a solid form, the light would enforce its own laws upon it. It molded the matter in its own likeness, which was like an undulating light wave. Then the form grew dense. The light had to adjust itself to what was stamped on that form by the external laws of nature, but it remained the master of matter and form. I understood then that the light was the soul. It was in charge of the matter. It created its body, neither male nor female, but gave it qualities common to both. For the light soul itself was at once both male and female. In itself it bore these two natures. Its male element was related to that which we call Will, its female element to what is designated Imagination. The body then was androgynous, which reflected the soul.

Then I saw that reproduction in these ancient times was not by an external stimulation but by imaginative internal stimulation. In other words, people reproduced by manifesting what they imagined.

Soon the powerful influence of external Earth forces challenged the imagination, making it impossible to procreate with only internal female imagination. The soul could no longer pour its entire force only into the androgynous body. The soul needed an added masculine form to make the power to procreate, but also needed to retain within itself the force of both male and female.

Then I remembered seeing the physical separation of the sexes (Eve being born out of the rib of Adam), which occurred when the Earth attained a certain condition of density. Though the bodies separated, the soul remained androgynous in both the male and female body. Thus, the attraction of male to female, or male to male, or female to female is the soul attracted to the other half of its androgynous self in order to be whole again.

I saw the density of matter partly check the power of reproduction. When the androgynous soul took on an exclusively male or female form, it lost the possibility of reproduction through imagination. Cooperation with another body of the opposite gender force was necessary in order to produce a new human being.

I will never forget my meditation, my imaginative explanation of soul essence. It has served me well in these modern times of experimentation and revelations regarding transgender identification. We are all androgynous in varying degrees because the soul is. Our bodies should be reflecting our soul's identity.

WHEN I walked into the Ritz in Madrid, I knew I had been there before (in this lifetime, I mean), but I couldn't remember how, when, or why. The staircase was beyond even Gloria Swanson's in *Sunset Boulevard*, calling to mind the ornate style of the Golden Age of movies, which was probably why I remembered it as a setting for a film premiere long ago when I was young. My past in Hollywood is distant to me now. I have difficulty being called words like *iconic* and *legendary*. I'm totally involved in the present struggle of whatever day-to-day events are occurring around me. I don't like sitting around recalling career highlights from my past. And that's what I imagine "icons" and "legends" are expected to do!

I had been to the Prado long ago and didn't even recall that. I revisited its glorious and priceless treasures. What an extraordinary trek into human art history. I was struck by the fascination that the historical male artists had for the male anatomy. So many paintings celebrated male nudity. I, being too forthright as usual, wondered aloud to another tourist standing next to me, "Were all these painters homosexual?" His answer: "No, they just didn't get around to the female form for another few centuries."

The idea of human gender, of male and female (yin and yang), has always been of deep interest to me. Even more so after the past-life regression in which I remembered being androgynous. I had male sexual organs but also could give birth through a birth canal. I was balanced and happy, with equally expressed masculine and feminine characteristics—yin and yang. It was during the Lemurian-Atlantean time period. For some reason, I desired to be able to objectify the other half of myself. I wanted to observe one part of myself, not experience it. I wanted to be all one thing, not equal parts of two. I remember agreeing to a new human idea of "gender division" whereby I could separate myself in half but would have to choose either a male or a female body in order to have a spiritual home for my soul. I chose a male body and my soul mate (souls are equally androgynous) chose the female half.

We achieved the gender division with the help and spiritual power of seven high Initiate priests who officiated over the process, one high Initiate priest for each of the energy centers (chakras). The process was possible because of the high spiritual power of thought manifestation which we had achieved. We lived more with manifested mind pictures than intellectually reasoned thought. I remembered thinking that thought itself must have gone through evolutionary stages depending on the values of the third-dimensional reality.

After experiencing gender division and the reality of two separate sexes, we defined ourselves as bisexual because we still possessed our androgynous souls but were attracted to the other half of ourselves as well as the same sex.

Is this memory of our original sexual experience what so many human beings are suddenly recovering in today's revolution in how we think about gender? Are the gay, lesbian, bisexual, transsexual people who are making headlines just a manifestation of what the Bible taught us? Eve was born out of the rib of Adam (gender identity division), and both felt the desire to become one again.

Anyway, the great artists of the ages seemed to be fundamentally fascinated with the male aspect of their identity, perhaps because they understood that there were other possibilities than simply being attracted to the opposite sex. In any case, we recognize today that sex and gender are not so much about who we choose as our partners but more about complete identity— the balance and inclusion of both male and female. How challenging it must be for some fundamentalist-inclined individuals to contemplate being whole and complete!

MADRID'S AIR was dry compared to that of the Canary Islands. I remembered how hot it had been for me when I completed the Camino in July 1994. Since I had forbidden myself to spend any money during my Camino commitment, I certainly hadn't seen the likes of the Prado or the Ritz back then. On the trek across Spain, I begged for food, slept in *refugios* (shelters), and managed to keep from making friends, which was the most difficult aspect of the journey. Walking alone with one's own faculties and thoughts and feelings was a journey into my own capability for self-awareness, sustainability, and self-trust. I thought about that when I tried and failed to fall asleep at the Ritz.

The first day we shot our scene in a real airplane with real seats that reclined up and down, and real heat with no air-conditioning. The crew proceeded as though they were comfortable enough, walking on all fours over seats, across aisles, and laughing at our jokes about mile-high sex clubs.

We shot and rewrote whenever we felt the scene dragged. It was supposed to be a funny scene, but also it was the reveal of Jessica's character's terminal illness. I think we finally got a take that worked.

After the first day of shooting, I went shopping with Miranda. I was astonished at how much the luscious Spanish leather bags, luggage, and shoes appealed to me. I spent a lot. I was not on my Camino that day. I bought Miranda a bag that I also bought for myself. I wondered if she was still bad-mouthing me to whatever friends she spoke to back in Los Angeles.

Returning to the hotel, I joined the company on the Ritz outdoor patio. It was not a place for conversation and intimacy. *World Soccer* in Brazil boomed from huge televisions set up so people could eat and cry and scream and carry on all at the same time. On the screen, I was watching grown men cry and hit and fall down and run in circles and do whatever was humanly possible to direct a little ball into a net. The tremendous screaming audience in the stadium either cried or thundered their applause or disappointment at every move on the field. I found it difficult to get involved in the game. I felt as if I was watching something akin to the Roman Games while the world burned. Or perhaps the world wanted to watch the games because the world *was* burning.

Jessica and Demi knew the players, the rules, and the complicated moves. I knew nothing except that two powerful women were president of the host country (Brazil) and the country that won (Germany). The gigantic hollering, crying, chanting, bloodthirsty crowd was frightening to me. It was of one mind, with a winning and losing polarity and not much of anything else in between. Watching the single-minded, passionate, unified response made me think of films I'd seen of political rallies in Nazi Germany. So as you can imagine, I found it ironic that Germany won the title. I was relieved that two women leaders headed up the monstrous crowds. But would that help? Everywhere I went, people were watching the soccer games in Brazil.

The second-day shoot on the plane was more pleasant. The crew brought in an air-conditioning tube. We could breathe now but couldn't get down the aisles. No problem. This movie was making everyone an acrobat of some sort, either mentally or physically. There was no complaining, no temper tantrums (well, hardly any), and we were in a city where the crew had families and attendant diversions—but still no salaries. No one seemed to be able to sleep at the Ritz, and no one could figure out why. It seemed to me it was as if the walls were permeated with memories of the Second World War. I remembered the time I had been escorted to a fancy open-window patio to sit and enjoy Franco's parade down the Gran Via with his harem and retinue of soldiers and guards. I half expected him to look up and wave at me. Thank God he didn't.

The food and drinks on the outdoor patio at the Ritz were delicious and served with old-world formality. Other diners from various countries came to my table and basically offered me congratulations that I was still walking upright. During one of the luxurious dinners, unappreciated because yet again everyone was yelling at the television set, someone delivered a message to Andy: "Call Tyne immediately."

Tyne was rarely around, either day or night, where we could see her. I didn't know where she hung out. She had a young man with her who seemed nice enough but never said much. Might have been her lover. Who knew? Or cared? By this time I knew a little of her repeated MO. She "worked" from her room and always wanted better Wi-Fi, printer, and fax machines. People thought she was a liar, crazy, an amateur. Again, she was the one to hate. And yet she was the producer. Often when I saw her, she was crying or distraught in some hotel lobby. Frankly, I felt sorry for her.

Anyway, Andy got up from the table and disappeared. Thank God for the soccer game. He returned some time later with Bret, our UPM (unit production manager).

"The bond company won't sign off on Shirley,

because there was one paper you didn't sign," said Bret.

I didn't know what he was talking about and said so. "Give me any paper you want." I said. "I'll sign anything."

Bret was slightly hammered and smiled that smile that always meant trouble. It seemed there was more he wasn't saying. Indeed there was. Bret had been hired as a line producer. Because of our money problems, he had become the UPM. He was the man in charge of trouble. So Bret was in charge of the Spanish versus American crew problems; feeding us when there was no money for catering; avoiding Jack Gilardi's calls; explaining the need for deferment; avoiding all other agents' and managers' calls; avoiding the bond company; getting only one hour of sleep per night; and the suggestion that we cut the script according to how much a scene cost instead of what it meant to the story. In other words, Bret was in charge of managing chaos.

I don't know when it happened or exactly what happened, but what was reported to me after the fact was that he had apparently called our principal investor, Dominick Hollins, and screamed at him, "You fucking liar, cheat, shithead, you are ruining everything. I can ruin you in Hollywood, which I will do, while you are ruining our lives here. You send your fucking money as you promised to do, or I will email your personal attorney that I am going to let the entirety of Hollywood know that his client is purposely not closing—unless he does it by today."

I didn't understand the last threat, but what difference did it make? Hollins then reportedly threatened to sue Bret for extortion. Bret replied, "I'm rolling a joint in celebration."

Charlie, our transportation coordinator, who overheard the conversation, said, "Jack Gilardi can rip Bret a new asshole in seven minutes. Jack should be on radio."

I did my research on Dominick Hollins. To put it simply, he was a bit of a barracuda. But he was *our* barracuda, and Bret's threats were not going to help get us the money. Then I found out what seemed to be a potentially catastrophic artistic problem related to Hollins's money. I learned that Tyne had made a special deal with Hollins to get his $3.5 million. She said she would guarantee that a certain actress would be cast in the film, and she'd be guaranteed a certain minimum number of lines, and those lines could never be cut from the movie. Never!

Maybe Jack was right. He should go ahead and call his Sicilian friends. But to kill whom? Jack had, by now, forbidden Tyne, Michelos, and Lucas (the lover of the man I thought was Hollins) to come near me. Risking his wrath, I talked to each of them all the time. That's how I got the material for this book, which I was now seriously considering writing.

Andy returned to the table. "If you fly back, I'll go with you."

Angie, another producer, whose company had invested four hundred thousand dollars, was now potentially in real trouble. She had supplied all the equipment and the tax credit in Spain, and had convinced the crew to work for three hundred euros per week. Her father was a very famous producer in Madrid. This would not look good for anybody.

The DGA contacted Bret, Nick, and other members and told them to strike by the next day. Every day there was another reason to shut down, but no one left. It was as though everything was meant to be experienced.

Why do the crews and makeup and hair and extras and actors almost always stay? Why are they (we) so committed? Why does the movie seem to be their (our) lives? How do they (we) know how to deal with no money, no sleep, creative differences, eccentricity, stifling organization or stifling disorganization, death threats, future unemployment threats, and potentially real disappointment when the public doesn't like what we've done anyway? Yes, everyone outside this business is a civilian.

Do we like being in charge of our own debt? Are we creative dictators? Why will we travel anywhere and everywhere, never seeing home or family for years?

Well, we resonate to *experience* more than civilians do. We, as a result of traveling to shoot on location, have friends all over the world. Our relationships are more intimate than those formed in almost any other kind of work. We develop skills that give us control over our own talent. We are not owned. So much happens to us when we do our work: the universe touches us and we touch *it*.

So . . . Dominick Hollins was withholding his money until he was guaranteed that this actress would have a fairly significant role, which would never be cut. Ostensibly that would give him final cut of the film. No director ever got that (not even Spielberg). You can imagine the assumptions that were made about the relationship between Hollins and this actress. The one that I favored was that she was his Brazilian mistress and so this was how I thought of her.

Overnight, Andy went to work with his friend and savior, Ken Lonergan, to add those scenes for an actress they didn't cast and couldn't cut. I couldn't wait to see what talented, creative artists would do. Tyne didn't understand the position she had put Andy and all of us in. She never understood.

After we finished the Iberian up-and-down seat

scene, I returned early to the Islands. I think I missed the energy of Atlantis! Because I was a person of note, the Madrid driver took me to the VIP section of the Madrid airport. It was a lesson in Spanish security. There would be no way a GPS could direct anyone. It was a maze, a diversion, and a route so convoluted that a terrorist would tear his hair out. The Spanish wanted their leaders and famous people to be safe, all right. Premium VIP status didn't do away with confusion regarding my ticket.

My greeter said, "Do you want to board first or last?" I said first. She said, "Wait here." She then ran out onto the airfield and waved at someone. He couldn't hear what she said, so she ducked under the wing of the plane and bolted onto the field toward him. In the meantime, everyone else boarded, so I just waited and went last. I had been told there were no empty seats. But as we took off, I noticed four empty seats in first class.

Arriving back at the Islands, I talked with Michelos. "I want Bret gone," he said. "Hollins's money needs to come and he's signed."

Michelos recruited Miranda to go to Bret's room and reprimand him for bawling out Dominick Hollins. She did it. She told Bret he should never speak to a prospective client and investor that way. It wasn't good business. Duh?

When she came to tell me and Michelos about her encounter with Bret, she concluded by saying, "Bret should be shot."

Michelos offered another idea (caipirinhas may have been involved). He said, "Hollins's actress arrives in a few days. I'll kidnap her. She'll be my hostage and the company can have everything I get from Hollins when he comes to get her back."

"Would you please tell Miranda to stop saying bad things about me?" I said.

"No, you are my darling," Miranda cooed. "Without you I am nothing. My arm will be out to help you always."

Michelos said, "You see, she loves you."

"People have been doing this to me all my life, ever since I was a little girl," Miranda continued. "People hate me because I have a cool life. I'm successful, cute, honest, and have a lot of friends. What can I do?"

I said, "Someone's got it in for you."

"I'm used to being betrayed."

Michelos said, "We're going to close tomorrow . . . technically."

"Show me the money," I said.

"I have to go now and beg the taxi drivers for tomorrow's scene to keep working until I get some money to pay them."

I went back to my room to watch the news. ISIS took over two more territories; Obama had no strategy yet; volcanoes were erupting in Iceland; Hamas and Israel were still at it, continuing what's been going on for decades; Russia was playing with the invasion of Ukraine; and stories abounded about sexual depravity all over the world.

The Akashic Records say that civilized nations have a structure and an expression, as well as certain aspects of a psychic life, all of which have been stamped on them by woman.

OUR ACCOUNTANT, Mandy, had maxed out her credit card to the tune of a hundred thousand dollars in order to keep production going; Angie had kicked in sixty thousand, and Bret thirty thousand. They and others were the reason we could shoot. None of the other actors really knew this. I was glad I had agreed to defer. The production people had learned by now to never give a straight answer to any question. That was partially a Spanish custom, like the convoluted road to the Madrid airport's premium waiting room. To me, everything seemed patently unfair, but I felt like I was being taught a lesson. I just wasn't sure what lesson.

Bret was packed and ready to leave the production. The word spread quickly that he had bawled out Dominick Hollins and that Michelos wanted him gone.

The taxi drivers wouldn't work without pay in the scenes scheduled. So we went to green screen and shot on a soundstage. There were several scenes we could get that took place in the backseat of a limo. A smaller crew worked, and the situation gave Andy time to work with

Kenny (our screenwriter, now also working for free) on the eighteen pages of new dialogue necessary for Hollins to get us $3.5 million.

Tyne snuck onto the soundstage as well as Michelos. What did that mean?

Jessica and I sat in the hot backseat waiting for Andy's "action." Suddenly, my neck lifts gave way. With the heat, the glue melted and my neck fell. I ran to Mariló for makeup and Pablo for hair and sat down so they could repair the damage. The crew hovered, watching the magic of the repaired uplift. I hate hovering, so I gave them a dirty look. They backed away. Having people hovering while others repair a disaster that wastes time is my most despised circumstance in the world. *I hate hovering!*

Suddenly, I heard people screaming at each other. I saw Andy, Tyne, and Michelos on the other side of the soundstage, engaged in something serious. I asked one of the crew who wasn't hovering what it was all about. He said, "It's something about releasing eighteen pages of dialogue to the man with the money."

Oh my God. They were insisting that Andy guarantee the lines to Dominick Hollins. I heard Andy scream at Tyne, "You changed the male character of Carlos to Carlita and made her a woman and I now have to write eighteen pages for her so we can get the money to finish this thing. You are a liar, a cheat, and a manipulator.

Okay, her name is not Carlita, it's Flavia Cunt Face. How's that? I can write some dialogue for that."

Was this the kind of thing that went on in Atlantis? My neck lifts restored, I returned to the backseat. Jessica smiled and said, "Maybe we all lived in Atlantis and this is our karma."

We got our pages for the next day. I don't know how or why, but apparently the bond closed and we weren't going to be shut down. I don't know who paid for the day's work.

At ten o'clock that night, after work, I was wandering around the lobby. The tourists didn't notice me because I didn't have my neck lifts on. I looked my age. I spied Jessica; she was wandering too. We had a drink. Soon Andy joined us. There were many boisterous jokes about Flavia Cunt Face. I learned that our soon-to-arrive new cast mate's nickname was inspired by another actress with the unfortunate name of Flavia Kuntz. The real Flavia Kuntz had sent a taped audition piece to the set at some point. Our new "Carlita" was due to arrive in a day or two. Andy wouldn't reveal anything about her lines or the release of same.

Several people from the production office joined me. Andy leaned in and said, "It's bad form to tell Shirley anything."

I said, "Wait a minute. I need to know the truth.

So does everybody. Besides, I'll find out every-thing anyway, so screw your 'bad form.' "

The talk became a rerun of how exhausting this experience had been. They each gave individual examples of what they had been through to keep the movie going, and how it had brought them to tears many times. They expressed how difficult it was to keep their cool while negotiating for whatever was needed, for no money. They hated to ask people to work for nothing.

After each confession, Andy would say, "That's bad form." I'd tell him to shut up. The others thanked me for the opportunity to be honest.

The night went on until everyone left but me and Jessica. The two of us, now completely, staggeringly drunk, decided to engage in an open and honest evaluation of which men in the world we would like to have sex with. Too bad I don't remember a thing we said after that.

Miranda seemed to be behaving more and more like a little girl. The chaos seemed to bring out her infantile qualities. While she was still very efficient and kind and "adoring" to me, I wondered if she might have several other personalities inside longing to come out and play. She was truly an enigma to me. She made it obvious she liked champagne and "wanted to get laid" and soon began wearing little Daisy

Duke shorts and halters. I decided to be entertained by her instead of anything else. Besides, I depended on her for everything. I needed to stay sane and she was good at keeping my life in order. And despite everything, I actually liked her.

We've become self-conscious
in a world ruled by our senses.

WE LEFT for another location in Las Palmas. Andy delivered a seven-page scene to Jessica and me, but there was no time to rehearse. We thought there was too much crying and too much dialogue. Jessica was usually concerned with whether she'd be funny. I was concerned with whether I could remember my lines.

The restaurant where we were shooting was very hot, torturously hot. Whenever I'd blow a line, Andy would yell out which line came where—guaranteed to screw up my memory. It was too mathematical, so I yelled at him, "Why don't you let me try acting!"

There were huge crowds outside watching us through the windows as we tortured ourselves. Because we didn't have trained ADs, Jessica and I never knew where to go after each scene wrapped. More often than not an untrained AD led us into the crowd. I must have said, "Where do I go?" a hundred times a day. I soon began dreaming of not knowing where I was supposed to go. Maybe I should go back to Atlantis?

July 4 came. I remembered that July 4 had been the day I completed the Santiago de Compostela pilgrimage. Today was Independence Day in America and we, as a country, were in trouble. I compared in my mind the rigors of our movie with what was occurring at home. In both cases, the patience required to tolerate the lack of personal leadership and coordination and organization was beyond the pale.

Was democracy not working? Was democracy itself the problem? A movie set couldn't be democratic and work. Maybe a country couldn't either. I knew Churchill thought that democracy wasn't much but was the best we had. Was that good enough?

There is no leader anywhere in the world today who was not in Atlantis.

We live in the New Atlantis.

Humans desired to receive
impressions from without.

They became self-conscious and
found pleasure outside the soul.

They had urgings that
were not soul-guided.

That was the beginning of
Good and Evil.

I WALKED into the foyer of the small hotel in Las Palmas that was our base camp. Tyne was sitting there, sobbing. Her eyes were wet and slightly insane. "I can't go anywhere without being treated like trash," she said. "I'm completely broke. I've been on this thing for seven years." She sobbed about her journey, the shame she felt over her mistakes. How she didn't know enough. Again she said she'd lost ten pounds. She had no hunger, only pain. She believed in the script. "Our casting director sent out the script with Carlita instead of Carlos. Everyone got confused. The investor insisted on the lines for his friend."

She didn't even cop to the fact that *she* changed the name of the character. She wasn't lying, really. She blamed the casting director for what she did. She honestly didn't understand what she had done wrong. She seemed to be solely oriented to the goal of getting money regardless of how she did it. But what was the difference between her goal-oriented value system and what studio bosses and CEOs on Wall Street did every day? The little people were being ignored, sometimes destroyed, and that fact was always irrelevant to those with money.

I left Tyne with some words of comfort and a hug, which didn't go over very well with those who saw me hug her. I didn't want to be late for our night shoot in the mountains.

We drove to the location in the hills. The Canaries were all hills and mountains. (My research informed me that another Canary volcano, Teide Peak on the island of Tenerife, had been two times higher in the Atlantis period.) The roads we took were U-turns all the way to the top. No signs or directions. Manuel knew where he was going, but Jessica's driver didn't. I wondered how long it would be before an eruption occurred.

The towns and villages on the island were built into the sides of mountains and hills as though the people were avoiding proximity to the sea as much as possible. I rarely saw anyone walking the winding road. People seemed to either stay in their hillside abodes or congregate in the bars and restaurants in town. I thought about renting a house for a few months to absorb more of the ambiance of what it all used to be, prehistory. A few of us noticed that we were sometimes dizzy for no reason. We couldn't sleep because our minds drifted into some other reality instead of sleep. Some of us would touch a glass or a plate and it would shatter. We were tired but couldn't rest; we were hungry but couldn't eat. We knew our lines but couldn't always remember them. We talked among ourselves about the tampering of our memories. Were we supposed to remember something about where we were that was more important than our lines? We would fall asleep while waiting to be called to set. Sometimes we'd fall asleep while an adjustment was made in the lighting. I thought so often of the gentle giant I had seen in the Caldera. He seemed so calm, so totally amalgamated with the trees and nature that surrounded him. Yes, he was out of another time, but I truly saw him *now*.

For some reason the Lost Islands were spoken of with great secrecy after the deluge because their inhabitants possessed superhuman powers. They were the last direct descendants of the gods or divine kings. The "gods" were supposed to be visitors from the Pleiades or the Seven Sisters constellation. To divulge the islands' whereabouts was punishable by death. Theopompus spoke of the Phoenicians sinking their own ships to make inquisitive foreigners lose all trace of them.

The gods of Olympus (the Pleiades) were said to possess the seven personalities of the 1) intelligent powers of Nature; 2) cosmic forces; 3) celestial bodies; 4) gods; 5) psychic and spiritual powers; 6) divine kings on Earth; 7) terrestrial heroes or men. The knowledge of how to discern the seven personalities belonged at all times to the Initiates. Those seven personalities (gods) were said to have incarnated on Earth four times. After that they became *human* kings and rulers.

Billy Connolly was comfortable in Atlantis. He wandered, as if it was his job to wander. I admired him so much for his talent to blend into nothing and everything. He rarely spoke unless spoken to, and then his rhetoric was cruelly brilliant. He was wickedly funny in his sarcastic evaluation of what was going on. Because he was usually so stone-faced, we would wait in anticipation for him to speak and thereby shatter the polite expectations of normal social intercourse or chitchat. Billy never chatted. He announced what he observed and blew polite conversation into pieces. His face was immobile as he devised ways to utter, without emotion, the cruelest, most filthy sentences about whatever was on his mind. He was a master comedian at delivering underdone shock. When we did scenes together, he was totally equal, unselfish, and without competitive instincts.

Acting with a partner on-screen is an endeavor like no other. There is vanity involved which, when your partner is a man, is usually relegated to the woman—but not always. I worked once with an actor who made faces to me during a dramatic scene when he knew his face wasn't on-screen—and he wasn't gay. I never could figure out what that brand of competition was about. When you're doing a scene with an attractive, good-looking man who is even-tempered and is concerned about both your performances and the real story you are telling, you usually fall in love. At least I usually did. There is nothing like the equality of intimacy or the intimacy of equality. Add to that the number of hours you spend together in that state of being while waiting for the next setup to be lit . . . In fact, the actor doesn't have to be good-looking—just honest about his feelings, his self-consciousness, and his respect for those same things relating to anyone else. Of course, you don't often find these qualities in actors who have had to brazen their way to the top! I always fell for the man who didn't act his intimacy but instead had the courage to *allow* it to be seen.

Screen acting in itself is an exercise in intimacy because you know the camera will see and reveal any emotional chicanery.

Working with women, for me, has never been about competition. It's more about the story and the humor we hoped to find in sharing the dilemma of being working women—with or without each other. I love working with women because we are naturally more revealing about ourselves. In those circumstances, the time spent in between setups is the most fun and the most astonishing in its substance. Actresses are a true revelation to me because they don't conceal their flaws. They openly exchange feelings about their own vanity, their terror at being seen deeply, and their opinions of the men who have a problem with the red light being on (the camera is rolling).

There are some actresses who reveal nothing of their true selves and proceed to demolish every trace of humanity in their vicinity. They take down other actresses, actors, the prop man, the producer-director-writer, and even the grip who isn't paying attention and could care less. That kind of actress won't be around long.

As we wound our way up the hill to a hotel that used to be quarters for farm animals, I thought about my past in this theater of life. What assures longevity? I never really *burst* off the screen and became a megastar. I don't believe I was really interested in achieving such a circumstance. I preferred to do the best I could and still have enough privacy to investigate those mysteries of the past that somehow made us what we are today. How many pasts were there? How many more would there be?

I loved the experience I was having on the

movie with the humor of the cast, the director, no money, little organization, cultural miscommunications, etc. But what I loved as much was being on the islands that used to be Atlantis. *That* was my reason for getting on the plane in the first place and for staying once I got there.

The Canary Islands were not named for birds. They were named for dogs (from the Latin *canis*) that were native to the islands, as were the islanders themselves. Despite living on islands, they did not often use boats, so greatly did they fear the sea and the legend/memory of their former homeland being swallowed by the ocean.

Once when I was in Hong Kong visiting a bookstore, I was perusing a shelf full of books when a book fell on my head from above. I had not touched it or bumped into the shelf; it came right to me as though someone thought I should read it. Called *A Dweller on Two Planets*, by Phylos, it contained material about Atlantis channeled by a man who reported on what he remembered from a lifetime then.

I remember well my feeling when the book literally fell off the bookshelf. I was about twenty years old, not at all interested in a lost civilization called Atlantis, and had not thought about reincarnation at all. I just knew instinctively that I should hold on to this book and one day I would understand it. Twenty years later I became interested in channeling and the lessons of Atlantis.

Hopefully, we have learned the lessons from its demise.

One of the most eloquent of truths relating to *A Dweller on Two Planets* was what Phylos said about our present-day knowledge. Knowledge is power, he said. But then in relation to having lived many lives, he said, "Thine own powers are not matters of heredity only, but recollected acquirement of thy past lives, also to give thee a hint of profit, to wit: We are with all we have seen, we do with all we have done, and we think with all we have thought."

Phylos goes on to explain that first came the Word—that is, sound. From one type of vibration everything else follows. A very low rate of vibration may be felt; an increase of vibration may be heard. For example, we first feel the pluck of a harp string, but then if its vibration is increased, we hear its sound. Following sound is first heat, then light. Light varies in color, as sound does in tone. The first color of light produced in the visible spectrum is red, then orange, yellow, green, blue, indigo, and finally violet. After violet, a further increase in vibration produces white light. Even more gives gray. Even more extinguishes light, replacing it with electricity. An ever-increasing voltage or vibration will produce psychic power. The laws of the physical world continue inward to their spiritual source.

The difference between types of matter, whether gold, silver, iron, lead, sugar, or sand, is not in the matter itself but comes from the degree of dynamic vibration.

The Word was from the mind of God. From knowledge of the vibration of the mind of God came all the scientific triumphs of that ancient past age, and one by one they are reemerging today after their long oblivion, and tomorrow they shall awake in crowds, and press for rediscovery, until men and women, platoons and corporations and countries remember what they once knew. And yet, in their behavior all beings must temper what occurs with the spirit. We must not allow the march of physical discovery to outstrip the advance of the soul. For if by this the whole world shall be gained, what shall it profit if it lose the soul?

THE SCENE close to the end of the picture was to take place in a winery where our lives were comedically at stake. Santiago Segura was cast as Carlos. Santiago was the biggest media and film star in Spain, and he is an extraordinary human being. He didn't have a clue that he was acting alongside Carlita, who was worth $3.5 million to us. But he knew more about me, about our American entertainment industry—television, film, scripts, who was in power and who was out of power—than I did. He was entertaining to talk to, intelligent, funny, and well informed. I loved that his first name was Santiago. I called him Compostela and he understood immediately.

One thing Santiago didn't know was the trouble we were having with money and his character and the convoluted eighteen pages of new dialogue problem to secure our funding. I have a feeling that sort of thing wouldn't have bothered him anyway. He had better things to do.

Night fell and we were ready to shoot the scene with the new dialogue. All of us actors were sitting waiting in the green room, which was a canvas tent with a heater in it. This location was high in the mountains and cold, a decided change.

A woman, quite beautiful, was introduced to us as Rebecca. She was tall, dignified, and friendly. We talked among ourselves. I was dying to ask her about Brazilian stardom and Dominick Hollins, and find out what it was like for her to play such an important cog in the wheel of our movie. She spoke fluent English with an accent. Social amenities over with, nothing much disclosed, I waited. There was plenty of time.

Andy came in the tent and announced, "I had a good night's sleep, so look out!"

I couldn't ask in front of everyone whether Rebecca was playing Carlita or Carlos or Flavia Cunt Face or who.

"We're ready," he said. We all got up. I asked Rebecca if she had her lines. She did. I managed to keep myself from asking, "How many?" I wondered if there was stuff going on that I didn't know about.

"Let's stage this thing," said Andy. "We'll block it now and shoot separate scenes later."

Okay. Good enough. We went to the street outside where we were going to shoot. Andy placed Santiago and Rebecca on a balcony looking down to the street below. The balcony could have been on another set, it was so far away. Jessica and I were to drive up and get out of the car and be stopped by a ferocious gunman as we looked out and up at the balcony. We began. Neither Jessica nor I had any lines, so we weren't prepared for anything.

We drove up, got out, a ferocious gunman shot bullets into the air, and Santiago loudly asked, "Who are you?" Rebecca (Carlita) began a long harangue at Santiago (Carlos) on being disturbed from her sleep. She spoke rapid English, but neither I nor anyone else could understand one single word she said. The harangue lasted several minutes and contained more lines than I could count. After a moment of stunned silence, Santiago (Carlos) spoke again.

Oh my God, I thought, *how brilliant of Andy.* I didn't need to be told. He could cut away from Rebecca to Jessica and me, and no one would know that she ever said anything. Hollins's friend was in the movie, you could call her Carlita if you wanted, but what she said or how she acted meant nothing. The question of whether her lines were in the movie was satisfied. Whether they *remained* was another question: the argument for them would never stand up in court because the director always had the last word on artistic creative differences. *Don't mess around with show biz smarts,* I thought.

When I asked to read her lines from the script because I couldn't understand her, I realized that the new dialogue was actually very funny and she had done a really good job with it. Wanting to contribute some show biz smarts myself, I asked Andy why he didn't just subtitle her lines in English even though she was speaking English. Andy liked it.

We did maybe three takes of her and that was that. We all returned to the tent with the heater. Someone brought hot drinks. Now was my chance.

"So, you're from Brazil?" I asked, still convinced that she was both Brazilian and more than just a friend to Hollins. She looked at me strangely.

"No," she said. "I live on Melrose Avenue in Hollywood, why?"

I was gobsmacked. Couldn't answer. "Oh," I said, "we heard you were from Brazil and a big star there." I'm rarely accused of being diplomatic.

"No," she said, "I love Brazil, but . . ." She didn't finish. I didn't know if she had ever been there. She talked about how much she liked living in Hollywood but how difficult it was to get work. *Well, in your case, not really,* I thought. *Should I ask her about Hollins?* No, I decided not to. Perhaps *he* didn't really exist. Perhaps we were all having a past-life memory about the sinking of the lost continent, which according to my research severely affected Brazil when it sank in the mid-Atlantic. Funny how some events, even prehistory, are with us today! (For good measure, I later found out I was wrong about her relationship with Hollins too. She was just an actress he wanted to help.)

We shot the rest of the scenes in the winery without much of Carlita. We shot all night for two nights. By now we were all exhausted. Jessica asked who she had to sleep with to get off the Islands.

Now that we seemed to have solved the problem, Andy banned Tyne from the set. Apparently she had not only not paid the writer at all, she changed the wording of contracts consistently and in general drove the production office crazy. I could understand why everyone treated her so poorly. Would anyone ever work with her again? Would any of us ever work again, period? was a more operative question.

We were coming to the end. Jack began calling it the "miracle picture." Maybe he was right, especially if it worked.

With locations around the Islands completed, I called an acupuncturist whom I had known before in Valencia to come to the Islands and give me a treatment. He was famous for not just acupuncture but *permanent* acupuncture needles. I believed that the permanent needles I had had from him a few years before had been one of the reasons for my continuing good health.

I offered his services to anyone who wanted them in our company, but no one took me up on it. So for a few days he placed permanent needles in my ears, which stimulated acupuncture points to the meridians all through my body. It was expensive, sixty euros per needle, but effective. My ears were sore, but a lot of the time I find I'd rather not hear what is going on anyway.

I had lunch with the production crew. Angie had mortgaged her house; the others had credit cards that were maxed out. I thanked them all and said, "It was an expensive learning experience." They agreed and said it was worth it.

The last few days we shot in a magnificent library in Las Palmas. By now, all of us actors were extremely tired. I'm sure the crew was too, but not only wouldn't they show it, the act of admitting exhaustion would have only slowed them down—and that couldn't happen. There was no money to slow down.

Whenever we shot in a town, there was always a restaurant that made a deal with the company: the restaurant was rewarded with meeting movie people, while we were rewarded with good food. For the end-of-the-day meal our underfunded band of deferring players was rewarded with time spent among ourselves—our "we're doing it because we believe in it" family.

The prehistory of the past affected me every day. I was preoccupied with the mystery of how and why these islands were part of a catastrophic event that could easily happen again in other parts of the world. Each of us talked about how the world was falling apart and no one knew how to stop it. We wanted to go home but we didn't want to return to our same old known world.

I would look out over the sea that surrounded us and ask, "What can we learn from what happened here? Were we prioritizing incorrectly by being so concerned with material things? But how could we really live in this world without being paid? And what was the role of the female now since the male . . . um, yang of it all had screwed everything up so badly?

In reading *A Dweller on Two Planets* I particularly remembered a section on the role of the female.

In Atlantis, questions about the relative value of the feminine gender to the male were never asked. Females were considered equal in all ways and seen to possess exquisite understanding of the hidden, mysterious forces of nature and humankind. The nighttime, feminine yin was the balance to the daytime, male yang.

I uncovered an essay by Rudolf Steiner on the birth of consciousness and how male and female came into being. My first understanding of the prehistoric "otherness" in life came from reading Steiner's book *Cosmic Memory*. It affected me deeply because I intuited in my soul that what he wrote was true. *Cosmic Memory* was my first step into the big, universe-size truth of life. I won't quote him completely, but enough so that I can convey his sense of the prehistoric beginning of consciousness and its expression. I longed to know how humans were created. The hand of God wasn't enough for me. The Bible had said "gods" in any case. I needed to get some idea of who the gods were and how we humans came into being. I probably wouldn't have been so intrinsically insistent had I not been living on Atlantean soil!

People who knew of my interest in the "beginnings" brought me many books from their Atlantean mystical libraries. The rest I perused on the Internet. Technology was destroying *and* teaching the advancement of knowledge and imagination of the human race. I read that the gods (of the cosmos, namely Pleiadians, Arcturians, Sirius, and Sirius B) ushered in the molding and development of a human race. They were capable of turning the existing forces of human nature into courses that led to the formation of mankind.

Before Atlantis there existed a highly advanced race of Lemurians. I remembered my androgynous lifetime then and have written about it several times. The "gods" appointed a small number of Lemurians to become the progenitors of the subsequent Atlantean race. The environment was tropical (the land masses being differently configured then). These Lemurians, with the help of the "gods," attained the mastering of nature's forces. They were full of energy and understood how to take Nature's treasures to benefit themselves. Through the training from the "gods," the Lemurians learned how to cultivate fields and use the fruits of the land. They became beings of stronger will.

As humans progressed and learned of their own consciousness, the gods allowed and encouraged them to form themselves into small groups. To the women the gods entrusted the ordering and arranging of those groups. Women, by means of their memory, were given the faculty of utilizing for the future all the experiences that they remembered and had once known in earlier existences. That which they remembered yesterday was turned into a present-day advantage. They became aware that the same phenomenon would be true tomorrow. The arrangements of communal life came from women.

To women, the expression of Nature was spiritual and appeared in the form of psychic faculties and visions. Inner voices spoke to them from plants, animals, stones, the wind, the clouds, and the rustlings of trees. They "heard" everything that was alive.

From such soul conditions, a kind of human religion was born. The psychic element in Nature and in human life came gradually to be revered and worshipped. Some of the women of the time attained special predominance because they were able to interpret from mysterious depths the phenomena of the world. From them came a kind of nature speech.

The beginning of speech lay in something akin to song. The power of their spiritual thought converted itself to sound. The inner rhythm of Nature resounded through the life of "wise women." Other people gathered around these women because their songlike utterances were felt to be the expression of higher powers. With that, divine power was embraced among men. Speech had no sense of the spoken word then. Only sound, tone, and rhythm were felt. People drew strength into their souls from what they heard.

All these procedures were under the guidance of humanity's higher leaders. They had inspired the wise priestesses with tones and rhythms. In this way the women were able to affect the souls of men in such a way as to ennoble them. It was in this manner that the true soul life was awakened. As the Bible says, First there was the Word. And the word came from the Divine Mind.

I had heard about the Akashic Records and was now inspired to learn as much as I could about what they meant. Science, skeptical minds, and mathematicians would have a problem with the hard-evidence reality of the Records, but then, even science was admitting that there needed to be a redefinition of reality. As an actress, I could attest to that.

The Bible refers to the Akashic Records as the Book of Life. This book contains the entire history of every soul since the dawn of creation. These Records connect each one of us to one another. They draw us toward or repel us from one another. They mold and shape levels of our human consciousness because the Records are eternally alive with our behavior and thoughts, dreams, fears, and experience. They are celestial tablets which contain all possible forms of energy—material, psychic, and spiritual. The Records contain the knowledge of creation under the impulse of the Divine Spirit.

Steiner said, "One who has acquired the ability to perceive in the spiritual world comes to know past events in their eternal character. They do not stand before him like the dead testimony of history, but appear in full life. In a certain sense what has happened takes place before him."

The Akashic Records could be equated to the universe's supercomputer system. It is this system that acts as the central storehouse of all information for every individual who has ever lived upon the Earth. They contain every deed, word, thought, feeling, and intent that has ever occurred at any time in the history of the world. The Records are alive and have a tremendous influence upon our everyday lives, our relation-ships, our feelings and belief systems, and the potential realities we draw toward us. Upon time and space is written everything that ever was.

The computer age has revolutionized the globe. No segment of any society has gone unaffected. The amount of information that is stored is unfathomable. Yet it can't begin to come close to the power, the memory, or the omniscient recording capacity of the Akashic Records.

We were on our last day in the Canary Islands. Everyone was exhausted and looking forward to leaving, having a rest, and catching up on our "real" lives before we made the sojourn to New Orleans, where we had a week of shooting left because Jessica would be busy with *American Horror Story* at the same time.

I watched myself count my flowered tops, boots that fit, and jeans that were elasticized. Our wardrobe mistress had been talented and conscientious about putting aside the pieces of wardrobe that I and the other cast members wanted to purchase for ourselves when we left the Lost Continent. After a present-day experience and a long-past understanding of the damage that materialism could do, I found myself laughing at how materialistic I still was. I needed more flowered tops and boots that fit? Please. I couldn't fit everything into my closets now. Why is it that women love new clothes and shoes and the right-fitting blue jeans to the point of losing all reason and self-control? That was not how I saw myself, yet I seemed to care more than I knew about how other people saw me!

My life in stylish clothing was strictly about the wardrobe I accumulated in "reel" life. In my "real" life it was sneakers and gym pants. I never cared how I looked anyway. If I wore the fabulous-looking and perfectly fitting boots more than ten times a year it would be a lot, unless I traveled with them. And beautiful flowered tops that were tropical weather items meant I would be dressed up—less than ten times a year in daylight, different for dinner. And blue jeans that fit tightly? I always felt I was too fat anyway, so they were uncomfortable to lounge around in, and I couldn't breathe around the waist!

All of it looked wonderful for a few minutes in front of a long wardrobe mirror. But for life? I knew better but bought them anyway and would do anything to ensure that the airline didn't lose my luggage, never mind my passport or money. No, I wanted my clothes to be safe. Why? I had asked myself this question so many times with no answer that I was seriously considering wearing a lovely wrap-around dress that, to my eyes, was like a celebration of each of the seven chakra colors. I had jewelry to match and would never again have to worry about having the right thing to wear. It would be my flattering Spiritual Age Atlantean uniform, and I could wear flat shoes. Then I would picture trying to tuck my legs under me, or sitting like a man (my favorite sitting position) with my ankle on top of the opposite knee, and the floating, lovely robe was away in a drawer.

As I grow older, I see many more women dressing androgynously. They seem to want a wardrobe that guarantees they will get no attention. I like that. I'm finished with feeling, *I must dress like a movie star* (which to me means chic but not flashy). People say they like to see me that way because it's pleasant for them to recall the Golden Days of Hollywood, but frankly it takes too much time and trouble. Chic is not easy. It requires a slender body and well-matched everything else. Too much time and trouble.

As I was packing the flowered tops, elastic jeans, and well-fitting boots, I got word that there was a final press conference. Jessica and Demi didn't want to be a part of it because they would be asked about their personal lives. I didn't care. There was not much people didn't know about me anyway (at least that's what they think).

So there I was: What should I wear to a press conference where I would be photographed by photographers from all over Europe?

I went as I usually do, for comfort. Loose ("forgiving" they call it) black pants, a looser tee shirt, and a very, very loose, long-sleeved hanging jacket with beautiful brocade decorations. I figured the colorful brocade would deflect from what I didn't want seen. Naïve, stupid, and in denial. I looked like a swinging tub with no indentations. But that was not the worst part. My hair was a mess from wearing wigs and no time for dyeing. The movie wig was being packed with the matching wardrobe. I had one wig I had thrown in my suitcase—I don't know why. My head hurt from the chin lifts and itched from the heat. I slapped the wig on and didn't bother to secure it on each side or from the top.

I made my way to the big patio feeling relatively secure with how I looked. It was a good thing there were no mirrors or reflecting surfaces before I got to the table with microphones. Everyone applauded. I was an "icon," a memory from better days, and I was still walking upright and working. Press and photographers and cameras and the Internet were out in big numbers. The lying producers made excuses for Demi and Jessica, saying they were filming in another location. It was up to me to hold down the fort.

The questions came: "Did you like the Canary Islands?" I answered I had always wanted to go back to Atlantis. "Why are you still working?"

Because I have nothing else to do. "Do you like the Spanish?" Yes, except for the way they answer questions with questions. "What was the Rat Pack like?" The likes of them will never come again. "Will you walk the Santiago de Compostela Camino again?" I could barely walk to this press conference. "Will you come back and shoot here again?" I think that's what I'm doing. "Do you think we've all lived before?" That's up to you. I know I have. And I recognize some of you who sank with me.

I was having a good time with the questions. I've always liked press conferences because members of the press are the most intelligent group of humans you can be with. Thomas Jefferson was right, in my opinion, when he wrote, "Where the press is free and every man able to read, all is safe."

I noticed that some of the photographers were coming closer and closer to me. Then I got a glimpse of myself in the monitor of one of the cameras. My unsecured wig had ridden way up above my eyebrows. If I bent over, it would fall off. I thought quickly. If I pulled it down in position, everyone would know it was a wig. If I didn't, my face and forehead would continue to look like a bulbous light bulb with no hair decoration. I wanted to die. Just then, someone asked me if we had had any money problems on our shoot. I reared back and made a face which was duly recorded by every camera there. I just laughed and said, "Thank you, but I have to go pee." I got up, thanked them, and left.

Of course the picture around the world was my face with no hair around it and a wig that looked as though it was ready to take off and fly. I wondered what the women on the Lost Continent did when their hair was a mess in front of a lot of people. Androgyny seemed like a better and better idea to me.

I was sad going to location for the last scene. Manuel, my driver, was sad too. But when I arrived, we all made jokes about really going to the airport soon. In between setups, I posed for pictures and signed autographs. Then the last shot was over. I thanked the crew deeply for their extraordinary commitment and hard work, despite the lack of *dinero* (money and salaries). They clapped loudly, wished me love and thanks in return.

As it is in moviemaking, that was it. Over. No more early calls, no more "What do we cut to save money?" discussions. We took more pictures, signed more autographs, shook hands, and gave each other hugs all around.

Then . . . I was alone in my little room that served as a dressing room. I took off my wig and stared at my distraught hair. I wiped my face clean of the makeup. Got in the car, and Manuel took me back to the hotel. We exchanged gifts (his to me being a gift from touristy Atlantis). He would go back to his security work. One more time he turned to me in the backseat and said, "I hope I do a good job," in English. "Yes, you certainly did," I answered. "And I hope I have done a good job too." I meant that more than he could imagine.

Then I had a long farewell lunch with Michelos. He spoke of how difficult independent film-making had become, but he knew that's where the good scripts would see the light of day, and where actors could win awards because they had good material. He spoke again about the money he had had to personally borrow with interest. He spoke of how difficult this time had been on his family. He hadn't wanted them to see what he was going through. He said our film had probably birthed a film industry on the Canary Islands because we were available to regular people and friendly. He said he wanted to create a lending company. I thought that was smart and told him he could only work with people who didn't demand lines for their friends.

Miranda packed for me in between tears that she shed because we were parting. She said she was going to take a vacation in Morocco. I wondered how long it would be before ISIS got there.

I said my good-byes to the hotel people because

I knew I would be out of there at four thirty the next morning.

I said good-bye to the rubber bath mats all over the floor in the bathroom, my yoga mat, the remaining chocolates in the dish on the living room table, the tangle of wires in the bed that serviced my iPad, cell phone, and owl sleep pillow, the flowers that lasted until the last, the various gluten-free crackers that Michelos had found, the barely sweet cookies that I devoured thinking they were sugar-safe, the fresh fruit the maids would take home, the swinging coat hangers that were now stripped bare, and finally I said good-bye to the balcony overlooking the silent ocean that held not only the secret to the fate of a sinking continent but perhaps the secret of whether our picture would sink too.

It had all been worth it to me for so many reasons. I felt happy doing something for love, not money. I adored the director and the crew who had stuck with us because they felt the same way. And I was reassured by my three-holed notebook, similar to the kind I used in the sixth grade, that preserved all my notes and memories and research of what it was like to "create" reality on the screen that represented present life while being far more interested in what had gone before, 850,000 years ago. The final sinking of Atlantis might have happened only 12,000 years ago. But its very existence spelled longevity.

Would show business itself ever last that long? Of course it would, because life itself was show business. Perhaps we in this world today were rehearsing *now* to repeat the same spectacular occurrence as the destruction of Atlantis if we didn't become more aware of our-selves and what we came from—and what we were doing to ourselves. Were we present-day inhabitants playing the same parts on a similar stage? Were we really the new Atlanteans, and were we still unable to write a happier ending? I longed for Shakespeare to come back and reconstruct a new three-act play world. When would we ever learn?

I fell into bed thinking about the one week we had left to shoot in New Orleans. The temperature would be ninety-two degrees at night. No windows were going to be open. The food would be delicious but would all taste the same after a week. My sinus problems would probably return because of the mold from Katrina. The TV would blast more gains for ISIS, America and the Ukraine would probably be at war, and the World Cup finals would continue to drive me crazy. It was all like the Roman Games: horror-themed entertainment on the air at CNN, and sports/ competition-themed entertainment on all the other channels. But now we were in the arena, not the gladiators. We had become the gladiators. I'm glad that at least I know I'm in show business.

HAMMOND, JUST outside of New Orleans, was a step into hell again. I had shot a picture there the year before and ended up in the hospital with a mold infection. I would try my best to look at the sunny side.

My best girlfriend/sister came to be with me for the week. Brit knew me and understood what went on at a location shoot. We stayed at a bed-and-breakfast that was right out of an Old New Orleans coffee table book. There was a big kitchen where I thought we would eat every night, but it always seemed to be closed. Our suite was down a long wooden walkway and surrounded by bamboo trees. Of course the windows were closed and the air conditioner on full blast. I have a problem if I can't open windows, regardless of the cold or heat or even rain and snow. I have often woken up under a foot of snow on my bed from the night before. Wonderful.

I unpacked, Brit and I caught up on our lives, and she loved that I was thinking of writing a book drawing an analogy between the reasons for Atlantis collapsing and the making of a movie that would possibly meet the same fate! However, she hated the fact that neither I nor anyone else would likely ever get paid our salaries. So we had discussions about materialism, naivety, work ethic, leadership, and whether the unaware human race would simply continue to repeat its past behavior.

Jessica stayed in the suite next to mine. She was doing double duty on *American Horror Story* and our film. She had also just bought a house in New Orleans with no bed—or anything else, for that matter—and had her hands full taking care of her dogs, which had been delivered to her from her other house.

We got right down to work. My nightmare was that the wig that had been established in the movie had not been packed and sent from the Canary Islands. If not, it would be called the eight-million-dollar wig, because it wouldn't match whatever we would have to replace it with on a reshoot. There wasn't enough money to bring the hairdresser from Spain who had styled all the wigs and hair in the film we'd already shot. The makeup artist came because she was married to the director of photography. There had been serious discussions about not being able to afford to keep the same DP, but I and others objected strongly to that because the new scenes would have had a decidedly different look without him.

The wig problem kept me awake until I saw the thing with my own eyes the next day. I knew how to care for it, so I could be my own hairdresser.

Jessica and I were handed a seven-page scene a few hours before we were to shoot. We bitched, but we coped, shooting in a restaurant with no air-conditioning because its noise would disturb the sound balance from cut to cut.

I can't describe the process by which I memorize my lines. I'm fortunate that with age I don't have a problem or need a prompter in my ear. Jessica was used to memorizing quickly because of her television schedule. Anyway, what we did was good, even though we had no rehearsal.

A trailer is a high-value item on a shoot because it's where an actor lives in between setups. But my trailer had a problem. Amateurs installed the air-conditioning system because they charged less, but they put the generator in backward. CO_2 was leaking into my system as the backward generator burned out. I told the New Orleans ADs. They understood the problem, but they just shrugged and said, "The three things you're gonna need here are wishbone, backbone, and funnybone." I almost laughed but I was perspiring too hard. Somebody had to beg for an extra thousand dollars so I would have some cool air in the over-105-degree heat. That somebody was me.

The New Orleans crew got right into "we're here for the cast" mode and were terrific. Andy was suffering from a cold he had gotten from having a few days' vacation in Paris on the way to New Orleans. His energy was still phenomenal and his focus undisturbed. I wondered if he ever got tired.

We shot many scenes in a private home and met the owners, who were also in a few scenes as extras. No one asked for lines. A dog next door *did* want lines and kept escaping from his owners and running onto our set howling. He loved the lights, camera, action, and the camaraderie in general. He loved to be chased, and the crew obliged when they could.

The crew didn't like the presence of the producers (Tyne and Michelos) on the set, but they were there anyway. A crew can smell an amateur by the way someone sits and watches what's going on. A film crew has seen it all and can give a reading on another human being's personality more precisely than any psychologist. Whether they will or not is another story. A film crew is the holder of many secrets, and what happens on the set stays on the set. I've said it before and I'll say it again: if our government sent a few professional film crews to invade a country instead of the military, they'd have the inhabitants in the palm of their hands in a few weeks. They are more professional than the military, more friendly, more focused, and they would be irresistible to anyone who wanted to be in show business—which is *everyone*.

Our crew was composed of people who had been borrowed for our weeklong shoot from other pictures. Some of them had not seen their families for months. But as everyone understands, there is something about our business that satisfies those of us in it like nothing else does, including families and lovers.

This crew from New Orleans was earning less than half of what their usual salaries were. Didn't matter. They liked the script and the cast. Do crews have stars in their eyes just like everyone else? Did a crew love being the power behind the stars because they understood none of us would be anyone without them? A film set is the kind of family you can't find anywhere else.

A neighbor across the street complained that the lights from our shoot were impeding their view of the stars. "We like to look at the stars," she grumbled. A crew member answered her, "Well, come on over and look at the stars that are walking around right here. We've got stars you can see up close."

Jessica and I had formed a relationship that had boundaries and yet was friendly and revealing. After work we often had drinks and inevitably our discussion would turn to some aspect of male/female relationships. One of our favorite topics was which of the men on the crew were desirable and which were not. I think we both understood that we had each had our share of seemingly desirable men, but did that make us any smarter about the future? Nope. She singled out one of her assistants who was slim, kind, and sweet. Not my type. I singled out a big, burly soundman who was within earshot and I knew was hearing everything we said. He seemed nice, and to his credit, he didn't react as he heard our conversation. Although, at one point he pointed to his ears when our talk became particularly quotable. That didn't bother either one of us. We knew the rules: secrets stay on the set.

I tried to initiate contact with the sound guy. He was too respectful. How should I play this? I saw him alone in a hallway on the house set. He was on a cell phone. I walked by, but he didn't acknowledge me. Feeling like Lady Chatterley, I strategized on how to involve him in a conversation without being obvious. At lunch there was a communal table where he sat with others. I sat down. He was slightly taken aback because I think he knew that I was flirting with him. We spoke pleasantries and ate. Then he mentioned what a fan his wife was of my books. Okay, we got the married question out of the way and the fact that his wife was "spiritual." He was a really nice man, honest, and didn't know what to do with me. Jessica watched every move.

After lunch (it was our last day), I was in my trailer waiting to be called. He appeared at the door. I invited him in. He had a card in his hand. He handed it to me and said, "There is a picture at Warner Brothers that I'd love to be a part of. Here is my information, if you can help." The location manager appeared at the foot of my stairs, peering in at the sound guy who seemed to be engaging me in a private conversation—something that is not done.

I blanched and thanked the sound guy and breathed in a deep, soulful breath of disappointment. I had been interested in him; he was interested in a job.

Jessica said, "That's what you get for flirting below your station." (She was excruciatingly right. I wondered if there were below-the-line and above-the-line boundaries in the theater of Atlantis.)

Being in New Orleans and the surrounding area, you meet lots of people who look at reality in multidimensional ways. It is a given that their city is mystical and full of the sights and sounds of other times. They glory in the fact that it is the most ritual-based city in America. They are quick to point out that, with Hurricane Katrina, these cultural traditions were spread across the United

States because so many people relocated to new environs. They are happy in the knowledge that their city's unique cuisine has sparked appreciation in cities all around the world.

The citizens of New Orleans understand that hurricanes have an impact beyond just the places they devastate when they meet land. The eye of Hurricane Katrina passed directly over their vulnerable city during a Bush administration (George W. Bush), and his standoffish behavior was seen as extremely insensitive and changed the way he was perceived. Likewise, when Hurricane Andrew, one of the most destructive hurricanes on record, took out much of Florida during his father's administration, George H. W. Bush was seen walking around in a daze looking detached. He did not declare Florida a national disaster area, the South did not vote Republican, and he lost his reelection campaign.

The ritual-bound people of New Orleans would say the goddess Yeminga took out both presidents. Yeminga is an African goddess who represents the ocean. It's not the hurricane-force winds that cause the destruction, it's the temperature of the ocean. Hurricanes and winds are associated with masculine energy. The goddess principle, which is the life-giving ocean, motivates the masculine winds.

New Orleans has always had a history of

storms, which are in some ways connected to the consciousness of the city itself. They say New Orleans knows very well of its own wicked, wicked ways but doesn't judge its own corruptions. It allows the cycles of nature to shift the consciousness of the population. With super-hurricanes, Yeminga creates a mass exodus so that her children can go out and teach other places about the importance of ritual celebration. The seeds of ritual consciousness are being sowed so that greater respect will be given to Nature and her cycles.

The well-known enjoyment of food in New Orleans is a ritual in itself. For example, most people know that appetizers stimulate enzymes for digestion in advance of your main course. But in New Orleans, it's understood that, in a similar way, ritual sacraments stimulate the chakras for the digestion of your enlightenment. Therefore, when you pronounce the name of the deity, in essence you are focusing your consciousness to receive the enlightenment. Enlightenment, they say, already exists surrounding us and is found in the ecology of nature. The ritual of pronouncing the names of the gods and goddesses enables us to feel our own preexisting enlightenment that we have forgotten. Our oceans are our conscious ancestors because that's where we all came from. Yeminga is the mother of all things.

Because the ocean was the beginning and end of all things, I wondered if there was research relating to Atlantis in Louisiana's prehistoric records.

Being in New Orleans stimulated my awareness of the innate theatricality of life itself. How could theatricality be so real? Even the poverty was theatrical. I remembered an actor on the film *Elsa & Fred* telling me that when his wife arrived at their hotel in New Orleans, she was greeted by a woman defecating on the curb at the hotel entrance. She was poor, probably homeless, and was not allowed into the lobby of the hotel. Such a scene would be considered too unrealistic if it were to appear in a movie.

As I watched the news every night, the actions of ISIS, the confused leaders of the world, and even the fear-riddled refugees escaping onto the wings of airplanes seemed to be pushing the boundaries where reality was concerned, but it was all real. I thought that pretty soon there would be cameras from CNN bringing the live ground fighting to national television, sandwiched in between pharmaceutical company commercials. They wouldn't need makeup or extras falling and writhing in make-believe death to entertain the audience to boost their ratings. They could save money below the line with a real-life war reality show.

I perused the prehistory accounts of the human race, books and articles written by people who were psychically talented to such an extent that they could decipher the Akashic Records. It made sense to me that Atlantis destroyed itself in similar circumstances to those that we are writing for ourselves now.

Why this made such visceral sense to me was what intrigued me the most. I'm as down-to-earth as a human can be in my interactions in life. I don't like bullshit or gilding the lily or lying for effect. I always demand the facts and proof of everything that occurs around me. So, given my basic personality, it is a magical mystery to me that I believe so much of what I researched then—because I don't believe in magic. What I was beginning to understand was a need for a recalibration of *reality*. Why are we so wedded to the three-dimensional evaluation of how reality is described and experienced? What is the boundary between imagination, on the one hand, and open-mindedness to truth that doesn't conform to our preconceived notions? Maybe one person's truth is another person's nightmare. Was that the definition of individual freedom? Every person has his or her own individual reality.

I noticed in my personal life that I was becoming more aware of life in other dimensions around me. I saw fleeting shadows out of the corner of my eye. I could hear the thoughts of others, which led to my interrupting them in midsentence just to save time. I knew when someone was pulling into my driveway or was calling me on the telephone before it happened. I could feel my doggies speaking to me and answering me when I spoke to them. I felt in touch with the old trees that surround my house in Santa Fe. *And* I knew I had a team of guides looking out for me. I'll never forget the day I questioned the truth of all of the above and went for a walk to think about it. I tripped over something and was about to stumble when I looked down. And there was a smooth rock with the letters TRUST written across it. I didn't fall. That rock sits with me on my bedside table as I watch the news for clues to how and where humanity is going. Does all of this make me crazy? I made a decision in my thirties that my "inner peace and knowledge" was more important to me than anything. If I feel I can't learn and resonate to the highest ideals that I possess, I will walk away from everything.

I think the film had become both my entertainment and my teacher, and so had the evening news. Did that mean that for me life itself had literally become theater? More than ever, I believe that Shakespeare was right. I like seeing entertainment from a point of view that I hadn't thought of. I like seeing life the same way. There is so much fun to be had in asking questions and learning. The laws of cause and effect, knowing that every action causes a reaction, were remarkably simple to me. It was possible to live by those simple karmic laws.

Killing and war are profoundly sad to me— not because people die. I had long ago accepted that the soul never dies, it just continues to learn. What is so sad is the interruption of the soul's learning curve. To me, we are alive to learn who we really are. That in itself has become an entertainment to me. Therefore, I am basically happy and content, always allowing my God-given imagination to roam free. Yes, experience is the best teacher. So, I believe that I have experienced all that I was researching. I was remembering, and my curiosity never dimmed, and I hope it never will. There is so much to learn and so much to remember. I am glad that with age my short-term memory is ebbing so that I can go further and further back in time and know *now* what I've learned over all these many lifetimes.

For a moment on the mountain Caldera I had experienced seeing a human being from another time who was at least ten feet tall, with reddish-blond hair and blue eyes. He was curious about me, kind, and slightly afraid of the present time he found himself in with me. Did he know that I had been reading about him in the Bible (the

Nephilim), which, by the way, was written in *his* future? So if all time exists now, as science says, why is it kooky or strange or even insane to look around, recognize what I see, and be entertained while making friends with it? I love the multi-dimensions all around me that I'm becoming aware of. Afraid of death? No, I'm looking forward to seeing if I'm right!

Since my encounter with my Nephilim, I came across a book about giants written by a researcher named Richard Dewhurst. *The Ancient Giants Who Ruled America* draws on four hundred years of first-person accounts, state historical records, newspaper articles and photos, and illustrated field reports. Dewhurst reveals not only that North America was once ruled by an advanced race of giants (called Nephilim in the Bible) but also that the Smithsonian Institution has been actively suppressing the physical evidence for nearly 150 years. He documents that thousands of giant skeletons have been unearthed across the North American continent, only to disappear from historical records. They were wrapped in fine textiles and dated to 8000 BC. There were hundreds of similar red-haired, blue-eyed mummies found in Florida, dating to 7500 BC. Had I been one of them and forgotten? Did we migrate from what had been Atlantis or were we already here?

I loved reading the history of the giant skeletons, learning the evidence that these giants existed widely some eighty-five hundred years ago. They had sophisticated cultures, were considered royal, had Caucasian genetic links, and left signs of cultural links all over the world. The fact that almost no one is aware of these giants today is a telling comment on the role played by the Smithsonian Institution and other institutions of higher learning. We rely on these organizations to explore, preserve, and offer insights into our heritage, most especially those aspects that hint at ancient advanced civilizations and possibly otherworldly influence. Why are these realities not put before the public eye? What have we lost by not remembering our ancient history? The stories of myth and antiquity are real. There were past ages as great as, or greater than, our own.

To quote Dewhurst, "We live in an age where we are hypnotized by our own ignorance, acting as if atomic energy and digital electronics are the heights of human achievement, patting ourselves on the back that we are the best and the brightest NOW." In truth, we are literally standing and living on the shoulders of giants. I wondered what their evening news was like.

We were coming to the end of our *Wild Oats* adventure, which to me had been about venturing into the distant prehistory of humankind and our cosmic neighbors.

So there we were, shooting the last scene. It was a funeral scene because my husband had died. Jessica, sitting by me, began to cry. It was *my* husband who died! It escalated into a full-blown, no-holds-barred, total nervous breakdown performance. She was Blanche DuBois on crack. Brilliant. What did I do? I played straight man to her comedy supernova—the same comedy that she didn't think she could do. She then said to Andy, "I want more footage!" I was flabber-gasted. She writhed around in Hollywood parody, claiming there had not been enough cameras on her and we should spend the time doing it over and over again. Was she really crying? Acting is a mystery even to those of us who are good at it.

Life was show business, and Jessica was eating up the scenery with her last scene on purpose. Bravo.

I made my "thank you for everything" speech to the crew, and I meant every word of my appreciation. Tyne cried when I hugged her. I mentioned everyone by name and again said that film crews should be hired to invade the necessary countries, not the military. They got it. There was applause, pictures, and heartfelt hugs.

Brit and I went back to our vacuum-sealed, ice-cold suite. Jessica left the next morning to go back to her role on *American Horror Story*. I would miss her.

The heat was unbearable, and although I had wanted to show New Orleans to Brit, we decided to get out of there as soon as possible. We had brunch with Bobby Harling, the writer of *Steel Magnolias*. He is a good friend who calls himself "the Tomb" because he maintains complete secrecy with anything you tell him. We spoke of aging, art, and the possibility of having lived before in ancient times and civilizations. His mother

had died a year before. She'd had Alzheimer's and it was distressing to everyone in the family. I asked him to try to channel his mother and write a comedy for me about a mother who has Alzheimer's. I wanted to play her because I had watched my mother suffer through the initial stages of Alzheimer's.

We discussed the meaning of scripted dialogue in anyone's life and performance. Weren't we all just actors performing our lines as though illusion were reality?

Just before I left, Andy sent me an email: "I miss you already."

I wrote back, "I love to act real, and I thank you for championing art above materialism."

Andy: "I met with another of our big investors (not Hollins) for music money but he slipped and fell on the marble floor of his palace on the way to his 747 jet. You know how slippery those palace marble floors can be. Broke his leg and is on painkillers."

Me: "How does the picture look?"

Andy: "Like a 25 million dollar film. That's why we can't have 25 cent music."

I wanted to email him back:

If you need food money, call Iberia Airlines; they'll take you to the Lost Continent of Atlantis with an empty seat in the middle for your comfort. I'll be waiting for you in my Atlantean palace with food for you— food you never heard of; I mean food for thought. Illusion or real, what's the difference? There's more to reality than you can imagine, Horatio.

With loving dreams from the past, or is it the future?

Shirley xxxxx

But I just wished him well and said I was looking forward to seeing the picture.

After the film wrapped, I went back home to Santa Fe. I needed to process as thoroughly as possible what it all meant. I felt the Atlantis material I had been exposed to was, in the main, true. But what was I to do with that? I decided to write about making a movie with not enough money whose location was the Lost Continent of Atlantis, which sank because of its overt addiction to gold and materialism. I loved the obvious contradictions and possible lessons within.

I now had three dogs: Buddy-Bubster, Terry-Tunes, and Trixie-the-Pixie.

So I sat down and wrote, as I always do, by hand, four hours (at least) a day or four pages, for about five weeks with my dogs beside me. I sat in a slumped position, because regardless of my body-science education, I concentrate more on what I'm doing than what it's doing to me. After six weeks I became my own pain in the neck. It was excruciating. I couldn't sleep, walk, sit, or even breathe without screaming pain. I called Dr. Leroy Perry, a sports scientist in L.A. who had treated me many times when I had injured myself dancing. He had gotten me through three long-term runs on the stage. He was famous among my crowd (stars over fifty in Hollywood) for making people well and functional. He said I should get a cervical collar immediately, wear it all the time, and get on a plane for L.A. so he could treat me.

The collar worked for a while, but I truly needed some more serious, even dire intervention. I was living on ibuprofen, and I have never taken drugs in my life. So a few weeks later I was in his office in L.A.

Dr. Leroy Perry has treated the best athletes in the world. He doesn't use drugs or injections unless absolutely necessary. He is a biomechanical genius who works mostly with healing and decompression in water. His theory is that hydrotherapy decompression in a pool of water is an antidote to the damage wrought by gravity. He warns patients continually, "Aging is a non-exercise in compression." He does excellent presentations about the results he gets from his hydrotherapy treatment. I will try to be as clear as possible in describing the experience—because that's what it is: an experience.

I was hung by a rope in a pool of water, in a position similar to that of people who are hanged to death. My head rested inside a harness that was secured with Velcro under the chin. The rope went to a pole erected behind me to securely hold the harness and my weight. I was instructed to gently flap my arms up and down under the water so that my neck would stretch out itself from its scrunched position. At eighty, my neck had enjoyed a long-term relationship with gravity. The feeling, when I first dropped into the water by my head, made me remember all the times I had been hanged in past lives! I breathed deeply and was patient with my memory terror until I remembered that water can save your life too. Gently, I flapped up and down and somehow knew that the buoyancy of the water would prevent me from really hurting myself. People of all sizes and weights had hung in this fashion in order to decompress, and no one had suffered an injury from it.

Pain was another story. I began a serious relationship with muscle memory. I knew muscle memory from dancing all my life. That is to say, when you learn a combination or a series of steps, your feet develop a muscle memory of what they are doing. Dancers know they can trust their feet and legs to remember something their mind can't. You can carry on a complicated conversation while doing complicated choreography because the body itself will remember. The lips have the same muscle memory. When you've sung the same song over and over, show after show, you tend to forget the lyrics. I just transfer my mind to focus on my lips and they will remember how to form the right words. It's a fascinating genius that the mind/body/spirit combination possesses, but it works both ways. Muscle memory remembers what it wants to remember, and what it doesn't want to forget! By that I mean when the traction of the decompression is achieved and you know the stretching out of many compressed tendons and muscles is healthy and structurally liberating, the muscle memory of the many years of compression from age and gravity insists on prevailing. The pain of muscle-memory genius has its way with you, as if to say, "We've been with you all these years bowing to gravity; you can't redo us because you want to be a healthier old person who can stand up straight the way you did when you were young . . . Here's the pain if you dare to rise above us and gravity: you are going down with us, compressed and shrunken and bent over like wise ones. We will give you memory pain and stay shriveled in your old memories until you give up or until you die."

Dr. Perry liked my humorous dramatic explanation of what I was experiencing, but he is also a serious sports scientist, and healing people's pain means more to him than anything else. To keep people dedicated to the discipline of his biomechanical health requires a colorful take on how to keep going with what causes you *pain*. No pain, no gain. How that idea upsets my spiritual beliefs is another story. For now, I will be specific about my daily life off the movie set and what I learned about my body and my soul.

I had never had any daily habits. I think it's because I love *not* knowing what life has in store. That was about to alter profoundly.

My pain from being hunched over writing was with me every day. I'd get up at the same time every morning, 8:27 a.m. All three doggies would jump on my bed and see to that. Buddy-Bubster and Trixie-the-Pixie would play-attack Terry-

Tunes, and Terry responded as though she's not going on sixteen years . . . adorable, until Buddy-Bub got too rough. I would then pat Terry's fanny; she'd get up on all fours and walk to her side of the bed. I'd scoop her up in my arms and take her out to pee. Same thing every morning. Since I'd never had any habits that I know of, this routine was a total breakdown of my cherished chaotic freedom. I'd eat one half of an English muffin (with gluten) smeared with butter and marmalade, or a dish of cornflakes or some-times oatmeal. I'd then scan my iPad for news, which always seemed to be ridiculously bad.

I'd then think about getting into my bathing suit and how distended my stomach was from breakfast. Too bad. If I was lucky, I'd need a bathroom soon and then I'd feel my no-booze/light-food diet was working. I put my bathing suit on first so I wouldn't have to bend over two times in the locker room. Then I'd put on wide-leg slacks because I knew my feet would be wet after the hanging pool and the shower, and big wide slacks would be easier to slip into.

Getting the right choreography for my daily life was paramount in saving time and energy. I'd tuck my underpants into my purse to be put on when I was dressing for home after treatment. Often I'd forget to include them—no problem. I got some rubber slippers that I wore because they kept me from slipping and falling on slick, wet floors. I tried to match the rubber slippers with my purse for some reason—old dress habits inherited from my mother: shoes must match bag. Scott (my assistant) packed towels, a terry-cloth robe, lunch food, and crackers because after I'd hung, I knew I'd be ravenously hungry, bordering on blood-sugar-drop disaster if I didn't eat. I picked clothes that were easy to slip into. I'd look around and remember my phone went into my slacks pocket, grabbed street shoes to wear after I removed the rubber slippers. Later I'd put the rubber slippers, still soaking wet, and wet towels plus the sopping bathing suit into a plastic bag—important choreography for the feeling of "in-charge organization." I trusted Scott had all his stuff packed and organized. I wouldn't bother to take a shower because I knew I'd have one in an hour.

We'd gather the dogs into the car so they could go to day care while we were gone. On Wednesdays and Saturdays a handyman came and cleaned the house, so he watched the dogs on those days. I felt like a working mother with three children and a bad injury. In the car Buddy-Bubster squirmed onto my lap. Trixie-the-Pixie fell asleep immediately because that's what cars were for. Terry-Tunes would be in her bed in the backseat. Everything and anything was okay with her. I put the visor up on the right because that was the sun-beating-down side.

I remembered all the days I went to work at a studio with the sun beating into the window on the right side. Then I'd sit in the back behind the driver. That's why I didn't have too much sun damage on my face. Driving into town, I remembered many early-morning calls—5:30 a.m. for months at a time. I still can barely understand how people can keep the same schedule every day of their lives.

We'd drive to Motor and National and get off the Ten freeway—I was lucky Dr. Perry's sports building was so close to the freeway—and I'd realize I was now one of those people I couldn't understand, keeping the same schedule every day.

I'd enter the dressing room hallway, take the same number of steps to the locker room, open the door, and take the same number of steps to my locker. I'd spend some time conjuring a more efficient way to undress and hang my clothes to save space. I'd feel so efficient that I already had my bathing suit on underneath my street clothes. I was adjusting to the low bar I'd set for myself!

I'd lock the locker, put the key hanging on a rubber band around my wrist, and proceed to the pool, where I would mingle and talk with other people who were old and injured and whom I would otherwise never have had an opportunity to meet and know.

There I was, hanging from a neck brace, my jaw clamped shut (but it didn't prevent me from talking with my new friends). I could feel my neck slowly release itself from its crunched, pinched, slumped, sinking position of eighty years. Many of the others, in their own neck braces, spoke of how the hanging traction in water had enriched their lives and consciousness even though it was painful.

I found a new appreciation for what people with pain go through. I found it excruciating, my days and hours centered around how long the ibuprofen would work. I was exhausted all day, every day. The film seemed a long-distance dream, yet I knew there was a connection. Yes, I hung in the water, and I knew I had now entered the senior phase of my life and would probably have to tend to pain of some kind every day from now on, because the exercises I needed to do for alignment and flexibility would now cause the muscle-memory pain to always persist. Dr. Perry couldn't tell me when the muscle-memory pain would come to an end. I hated not knowing how long!

I was living in a world of chronic pain because I was getting better, and I couldn't even imagine relief. I couldn't drive or go out to dinner or a movie. I lay stretched out on my sofa waiting for my doggies to jump on me so I could shift my consciousness to them and away from the dark horror of my neck. Perry said I would have to "hang" for the rest of my life if I wanted good posture and longevity.

Okay, it would be worth it. Nothing in my physical life had ever deterred me before, and I wasn't going to let it happen now. And I didn't want to retire.

I had agreed to do a benefit for the American Red Cross in Florida, and I had to present an award at the Oscars. Perry agreed that I could have a shot of lidocaine or some kind of pain-killer to get me through that. The shot worked: a week without torture.

I made a friend at Perry's pool who had serious connections and who lived in Florida. While I was there, he suggested, I should have stem cell injections. I knew Perry had had such a treatment and it had worked very well for him. My friend was in treatment as well and introduced me to the doctor in Florida.

And so a new field of study entered my life: learning about stem cells, which are widely believed to be the basis of a new kind of medical therapy.

Stem cells are the basic building blocks of our bodies, with the potential to turn into all the different cell types (more than two hundred!) that make up a human being. It is thought that under the right conditions, they can divide an unlimited number of times to create new cells throughout our lifetime, like a supercharged repair system.

The two basic types of stem cells are embryonic stem cells and adult (or tissue-specific) stem cells. Embryonic stem cells come into being only a few days after an egg is fertilized by a sperm. After dividing for a short period of time, those cells start to develop into the more specialized cells that our bodies will need. Adult stem cells can be found in various organs and tissues such as the brain, bone marrow, skin, liver, and muscles. Their main job is to repair and replace damaged or sick tissue.

The problem is that as we grow older, our stem cell reserves start to diminish (opinions differ on how much), and our bodies lose the ability to repair themselves. On top of that, environmental toxins as well as self-destructive behaviors like poor diet, lack of sleep, drinking too much alcohol, and smoking tobacco have a negative impact on the structures of our cells. For stem cells, stress is another bad guy. Stress—be it environmental, physical, chemical, biological, or emotional—gets in the way of cellular reproduction. (Not to mention basic human reproduction!)

There are all sorts of theories on aging, but whatever the reason for our body's decline as the years go by, the theory behind stem cells is that if we can replace aging cells with new ones, we can possibly stop or even reverse the aging process. Some scientists predict that, using stem cells, we will eventually be able to live several hundred years. Others say that biologically our bodies have the potential to live 100 to 110 years, but with the help of stem cells we might be able to reach a life expectancy of 130 years, and by maintaining a disease-free environment, we might also improve the quality of life for that long.

Theoretically, with every stem cell injection, you receive millions of cells that will continue to stay stem cells, so you have increased the pool of stem cells available in your body. But research also suggests that we have regulatory systems that control the number of stem cells in the body and that means only a very few of the new stem cells from the injection stay active. Other scientists don't agree with this theory, and people (including me) have reported good results from their stem cell treatments.

Stem cell science is still a very young science, and there are obviously lots of questions and numerous studies to be done before we can feel sure about the results of stem cell therapy. And that's why it's important for science to be able to continue to do this research.

We are but a cell with an imagination.
It knows neither boundary nor limitation. The cell cannot live in a hostile environment.

If our species is to survive, it will only be because we were smart enough not to criticize its imagination but to nourish it with our dreams and hopes. Science will follow.

—DR. LEROY R. PERRY, JR.

MY PERSONAL experience into stem cell injections was a circus.

First of all, the doctor was apparently brilliant and in the forefront of such therapies today. He was also a cabaret singer in nightclubs after work.

As I walked into the Center for Regenerative Medicine in Miami, I was met by the loud sound of Frank Sinatra belting out "Fly Me to the Moon" from a 1940 jukebox in the hallway. There were pictures of all the big show business stars who were the doctor's patients. So I reasoned that although the jukebox and music seemed unusual, show business–wise, A. J. Farshchian, MD, apparently knew what he was doing.

Nearly everyone who worked for him (nurses, orderlies, receptionist, etc.) was Cuban. I mentioned I had spent time in Cuba with Fidel Castro. People stopped smiling. No good. I never mentioned it again. The English that people spoke was another language to me. Other patients wandered into my room (no doors were shut). I didn't care, except that they wanted autographs and to chat about their favorite pictures. It was as though I were on the streets of Havana.

The doctor and his people explained to me what was wrong. It was the same diagnosis I had gotten from Dr. Perry. They assured me that I would have no pain after stem cell injections.

My friend Al was having his own injections, so I was ushered into an injection room across the hall from him. The doctor took fat from my stomach (plenty of it) and blood from my arm. He mixed the fat and blood. I lay facedown on the table and proceeded to get twenty-one injections into my neck. It is useless for me to report how I cussed and screamed with every shot. It was awful. Al came into the room and held my hand, warning me each time: "Injection now." I behaved like the pain pussy that I am. I don't think the Cubans had ever heard the mixture of curse words that I concocted. (I can't even take the pain that goes with a vitamin C shot.)

The torture over, I rested for a minute or two, then I posed for pictures with the medical crew and hugged and kissed everyone good-bye as Frank belted "New York, New York" from the jukebox. Al and I went for a caviar lunch. An hour later I was on a plane to return to California.

I went over the material written about stem cells and what one can expect. Accordingly, I adjusted to a few more weeks of pain.

Dr. Perry was surprised that I had done such a treatment, but he was well versed on what to expect. Also, he had had stem cell therapy himself after having been bitten *twice* by brown recluse spiders. I suggested he look into his karma with spiders, but his feet were "too firmly planted on the ground for that."

He'd benefited greatly from his own stem cell injections and had no problem with what I had done without his knowledge.

I waited for the stem cells to take effect. I did my boring ultra-scheduled water therapy every day, regulating my life and activity around the pain—which continued without any hint of letting up. Bathing suit, slippers. Warm water, driving and eating in the car, up at 8:27 with the dogs, lying down and writing. Bathing suit, slippers. Warm water . . . repeat and then repeat again.

Then on the tenth day after the injections, I realized *I was pain-free*.

My world changed. In fact, I didn't know what to do with myself. I was tempted not to hang in the water or go to therapy at all. But being an ex-dancer, I knew that water exercise and hanging should be a part of my life for the remainder of it.

Dr. Perry explained that the stem cells were replanting the garden of my system. I could feel it. I began to sleep more soundly and sometimes got ten hours a night. I laughed more. I became more patient. I moved more like a giraffe.

As the days passed, the pain didn't return. I didn't have to lie down four hours a day just to bear being alive. Then I noticed that I needed to seriously adjust to being peaceful and physically happy—not easy for an overachiever who wants to learn *everything*. My adjustment for a long and peaceful, happy life comprised moving more slowly, giving up impatience, not having a glass of wine at the end of a day, understanding the pain of others, and not becoming depressed at the evening news. Most important, I was coming to realize that most of what we humans had been taught as our history was not true.

As I hung in the water, I would meditate and have water dreams. It is difficult for me to impart what my Atlantean recall pictures have meant to my peace of mind and knowledge of times past. Why Atlantean recall gives me peace of mind is a mystery. I think it's because I realize now that all time and experience moves in cycles. There is no death: there is only consciousness experience. As I hung in the water, my mind wondered when we would ever learn the reality of cycles of change. Water is never in a permanent state. It is constantly changing . . . ebbing and flowing. We are 98 percent water, ebbing and flowing.

My mind stirred in circles as I tried to meditate and make sense of it all.

Are we Americans the new Atlanteans, as folklore teaches? If so, we seem to have learned almost nothing on our march toward democratic enlightenment.

PAIN, FOR me, had become my greatest teacher. Because my pain led me to a healing by water and stem cell regeneration, I found myself returning to the things that I visualized as being part of "the beginning." Where did I come from? Did I come from water? Was I once only a cell? Could I perhaps remember those things if I wanted to? Was my first cell the embodiment of imagination, which then imagined itself into reproducing itself, finally becoming me? And did my soul enter those cells to give me consciousness? Of course, I've always had a Buddha nature, so whatever answers I came up with would only be springboards for more questions.

I decided I would use the meditative environment of water to see what I could remember. I began to hang from my head harness in water and go into a deep meditation. I would ask my higher self to show me "the beginnings" and it responded with what seemed to be truth pictures. Almost like looking at a movie. It was enchanting entertainment. I had long ago given in to under-standing that we had each imagined and created our lives (past and present). But now, with the assistance of ebbing and flowing water as my circumstantial environment, I saw pictures in my "mind" that were enthralling, confusing, very informative, and in the end, entertaining—just like my life. I was the director, writer, actor, and *imaginer* of all my experience. More than anything, what I saw did not fit the description of facts because I didn't see people or animals or scenes as objective reality. I was experiencing facts of created truth. I was *inside* what I saw and experienced, so that I could *learn* from what I was imagining and creating. Imagination can be profoundly disturbing, but then, so are our imagined lives that we call "real." I ventured into the water-induced imaginings without judgment, and it was entirely liberating where truth itself was concerned. I did not feel I was going crazy.

My first imagining was that of co-creating, with God the Creator, a gigantic flying dragon who could move and travel anywhere. I was so enchanted by my power dragon that I made the soul decision to live inside it for a while. I became my creation. I wanted to experience what my imagined dragon was actually capable of. I felt how intimidating it could be, how awe-inspiring, how courageous, how frightful, and how controlling. My dragon experience taught me how to create many physical identities through which I could experience life wherever I wished.

Hanging in the water, I saw many pictures. Because I was so interested in the film I had just made and how it connected to Atlantis, I asked my higher self to show me how they were connected.

Fading into my vision, I saw a lush green and flowered garden. There were little elf-like people underneath the garden. I didn't know how to get to them. My higher self said, "Envelop everything with a pink-frequency light color and you will balance with them." In the light frequency wave I went below the garden, where the little people directed me to a giant waterfall. I let myself fall into the waterfall. The water opened at the bottom and I was in the air of another planet, floating. As I was floating I realized *I was* my flying dragon, watching the little people laugh at me because I thought I was powerful. Every now and then I'd land and the little people would come and sit on my wings and play. Suddenly I had an excruciating pain in my neck at the back. The little people sent me pink-frequency light and I felt better.

I felt myself try to remember when I first knew of Atlantis. I saw that time is not linear. It is a circle. I'm not the dragon anymore. I'm on Earth, human now, and I feel I don't want to remember, because the demise of Atlantis is so painful. Then I remember a house I lived in. There was no furniture. Instead there was a mandala from which I could meditate, imagine, and create anything I wanted. Nothing was permanent (like water, always moving). I saw crafts from other worlds above me. I often went aboard and I called the occupants of the crafts "gods." They said they were showing me the demise of Atlantis. The craft people want to teach me about the knowledge of color and the power of crystal energy. The human people on Earth had no knowledge or respect for the crystal power. It was operated and used for energy by the star nations people.

I saw the Earth from high above. I saw a crystal moon, which the star people said they had created to give energy to the Earth.

Then in the middle of the Atlantic Ocean I saw a gigantic island. The star people told me that it was the center of all energy for the Earth and was connected to each land mass, which would one day become countries. They told me that energy was to be used as power to create.

I saw a mountain shrouded in mist. I saw myself floating in and out of a cave inside the mountain. There was a light source inside but I couldn't tell where it came from. There were images of people, which I spoke to. They weren't "real" and yet they were. They were of a different magnetic frequency and they said they were from a different star system, so their physicality was not solid like ours. I could pass my hands right through them. I saw myself having "sound" conversations with them. But the sound conversations were not audible. The words and meanings resonated somewhere in my solar plexus as if I was supposed to feel the meaning, not hear it. We sat together and they told me stories about their home world. They showed me scenes of myself when I ostensibly lived there at some other time and place. I felt that I truly remembered the experience.

Then I was above the Earth again and I saw my mountain sink into the ocean. I found myself crying, desperate to understand what had happened and why. The star people said, "Every feeling has its season." I asked out loud, "Does God have both positive and negative polarity? Is all this destruction part of a plan?" They said nothing.

I saw myself as a power-hungry man. Then as a woman who struggled with being ignored. I was distraught. The star people said, "Your mountain was the feminine source. Since she sank, the feminine identity has been nearly invisible."

I asked the star people if I could see my soul, my higher self; could I observe what it looked like? My vision bleeding and morphing, I see a woman sitting on a golden throne wearing a golden robe. There are animals in her lap. She is calm, thoughtful, and lovingly detached. Ferocious wild animals snuggle to her face as she caresses and cuddles them. They come and go, sharing time and speaking with her. They don't fight with one another. They sometimes argue a little but then look to her for resolution. She smiles and they smile. They all seem to know they are equal. Now I see *I* am the woman. I am so happy with the animals. I see my arms stretched out and touching the land, my arms are so long. All breeds of animals take turns resting on my arms. Some people climb onto my arms but the animals don't want them. The animals tell me the humans have been cruel to them.

The star people tell me that I was one of the star people and participated in the creation of the animals out of the soil of the Atlantean earth. The soil was highly charged with creative frequency so new life could be made with the illuminating power of imagination. Several of us would create them and then swim with them. Food for the animals came like manna from heaven, from the star crafts. The food nourished every cell. The star people on the crafts were overjoyed to see humans and animals love each other. The star people told me that they were concerned that if they fed the animals too much, they would grow too heavy for my arms. The animals answered, "Enough for now. When we grow hungry again, we will look up and smile." The animals then would take turns with knowing the humans.

Suddenly I was my flying dragon again. I offered the animals and humans rides on my wings. I huffed and puffed, being theatrical as I took animals and humans on joyrides over the ocean. The new Atlantean city of Poseida was below us. I began to hear sounds, which became words. Different cosmic species of star people were building a city that was a work of art. Then I realized I was looking down at a creation that was 850 thousand years ago. The new creation was being constructed by many cosmic civilizations, each contributing to the new world—Earth—and I had been there!

I became aware that with the new civilizations from the stars there was no fear. They were without fear. I was fascinated that fear didn't exist. All life knew and understood transparent communication. Nothing was hidden. No thought was private. Thoughts were communal and shared, even though each individual was different from the others. Even the animals were without fear, so there was no competition for food. I saw that neither the animals nor the humans ate much. They were somehow nourished with an energy of peace. They existed on fruit—no meat at all.

Time didn't exist. Then some live communicator said, "Millions of years elapsed as the life on Earth was created." I saw animals stand up and walk as humans. I saw humans become animals again. The souls of each were experimenting with the various existences. They loved and understood each other because each soul had been the other at another time. I saw the star people revel in their creative handiwork as they assisted in creating life in their own image. Souls came from all over the cosmos to enter the physical bodies and experience life on Earth in a three-dimensional frequency. The new humans called the star people "gods" because they came from the sky and were creating life for them to experience. The "gods" themselves were searching for who and what had created them. As above, so below.

The weather seemed even and without turbulence. The star people understood that Mother Nature always followed the consciousness of the life on a planet, regardless of its cosmic location. If human consciousness was conflicted and turbulent, then nature reflected such a state of being. If the ways of the star people were peaceful, the nature of the planet they were inhabiting was peaceful.

The star people saw themselves as the teachers of the new "hu-mans." They taught art, science, mathematics, history, and technology. They were, of course, hundreds of millions of years more advanced than the hu-mans of Earth. They set up educational centers—centers for mathematics, for architecture, for writing, for music. The star people were impatient for the humans to learn more quickly. They took over the timeline for the expansion of knowledge on the Earth. I saw that for a while it worked. The hu-mans were anxious to learn. But the animals were not included in the educational system. With the passage of time (millions of years), the animals became completely ignored and feeble, engaging in more and more predatory behavior. Being isolated from the daily lives of the hu-mans, they lost the memory of how to get along without fear. Thus fear was born on the Earth—fear of loneliness, fear of isolation and abandonment.

I saw the complications of animal isolation from hu-mans and vice versa. It made the Earth unhappy, and as a result all life came under the direction of the star people. There was a marked decrease in transparent sharing and thought transference. The animals and the hu-mans became subservient to the star nations who were their teachers.

As I watched the events, I was struck by what the simple separation of hu-mans and animals had wrought. I wondered whether in the begin-ning the animals could just as easily have learned to read and write as hu-mans had done. My mind raced to the depiction of the Minotaur in Greek and Roman art. Were the people remembering a time when animals and humans were one? Were they depicting the equality of humans and animals, which had long since disappeared?

The complications of star-nations technology and the rush to teach humankind their knowledge was the beginning of the end of the Golden Age of Atlantis.

I watched more . . .

The star people had perfected the energy of crystal frequency. I saw that they could create anything they imagined with the crystal frequency. But with the emanation of isolation and loneli-ness came fear on many levels. Survival instead of evolution became supreme. No one really felt deep peace anymore. People began forming groups and fighting.

The star people erected crystal lines of energy in the skies that originated on Atlantis and reached land masses that would later become continents around the globe. The crystal lines fed energy to wherever it was needed.

As disagreements broke out with the elimination of thought transparency, the colonies of the Atlantean empire formed their own governments. I saw wars and skirmishes develop in the Mediterranean, South America, North Africa, Africa, India, Australia, Western Europe, and

North America. As far as I could see, the Orient was not involved with the dissolution of peace. They were another world, developed by a separate group of star nations.

What astonished me the most as I watched the spectacle of our ancient history was that Earth itself was the child of various star nations. The star visitors (the gods) created man and beast in their own images out of energies and DNA, water and soil and thought and crystal fundamentals that they were familiar with on their own worlds. I was haunted by what I was learning. My question was, Who created them? When I asked it over and over, they would answer by saying, "I am that I am." Did that mean we were all God, creating with our imaginations and wondering where each of us came from?

The star people were experimenting with life on Earth. They were exercising their power and began to have disagreements among themselves. The crystal energy lines and the distribution of crystal energy became the central point of manipulation and disagreements. The star nations had buried giant crystals in the "colony territories." They controlled the crystals but were now arguing among themselves and with the humans living in those colonies. The humans still referred to them as gods but were becoming more and more rambunctious.

As I watched, I somehow understood that eons

were going by in increments of ten thousand years. At the end of each ten-thousand-year period, there were Earth shifts—sometimes violent, sometimes not. But Earth itself seemed to be reacting to the unsettled consciousness of the people inhabiting it. I found myself asking, What does abuse of power entail? What were the star people afraid of? How does one have love, freedom, *and* cooperation? Everyone in that time had been educated to know that death wasn't real. In fact I saw many souls "die" and return to balance their karma, so to speak. I watched the ongoing dance of "what one puts out returns to the sender." It was a law of cosmic physics. It must have always been known to be the behavioral equalizer. And if everyone observed its rule, there would be no problems. It was a more taxing rule than the Golden Rule of "Do unto others" because it implied one's own punishment if one didn't observe it.

I saw the theatricality of human behavior. It was like watching a movie. As an audience member, I knew that the culprit would receive comeuppance before the end. So, if we each had always known this truth in our bones, why did we behave despicably, even in the Atlantean time period?

I wondered why the star people didn't teach fear of karma as a tool for cooperation. Wouldn't that force people to get along? No, they had problems with power and abuse too. Again, as I watched, I wondered about God, the Creator. Did he/she ever use fear in order to teach?

Suddenly, everything shifted. I was a man on the land watching Atlantis being built. My wife reminded me I used to live in the sea with long arms so that animals could rest and enjoy the water. She tells me that star people are making a new human race and a new land. The buildings going up look like tall, thin mountains reaching to the sky, so as to save land.

I was suddenly deeply aware of my lack of comprehension of time. What was time? I was seeing the past and the present inside a larger past. My neck began to throb with pain. I knew I was feeling the pain from even another time period far later than Atlantis.

I was in the Middle East. I was in a hole, buried up to my neck in the desert sand. There was a man buried next to me. I couldn't place who he was—then or now. It seemed we were lovers and someone was torturing us. I began to strain my neck so that I could rise out of the sand. My brain was functional, but I couldn't see or hear because my face had been pecked out by birds. It was horrible. As I looked back, I could feel the fear encased in my neck. I felt totally abandoned by God. I was being tortured because of my belief in God, and God was gone. My neck was on fire. Was this the reason for my neck pain now? Was I subconsciously remembering this terrifying event? I couldn't turn away from the bloodthirsty birds, no matter how hard I tried. My face was totally eaten away and I was alive. The pain in my neck became excruciating as I remembered. Why didn't God help me? I was being tortured because I loved God. Didn't he care?

Then I saw myself pass away, furious with God. Then I saw several incarnations when I had no spiritual faith at all. The memory of God's abandonment on the desert was with me for several lifetimes. Sometimes I had neck pain, sometimes not. I asked myself what was missing in me that my belief in God was so limited.

Then I understood. I was asking for God to save me when the point of being alive was to find the God in myself. *That* was the point to being alive.

As I realized that, my neck pain disappeared. The task for the rest of my life and lives was to remember the God within. Suffering would come from forgetting that. Would I be punished if I forgot? Yes, I would punish myself. Rather than the word *punish,* I would call it *suffer.* Without the knowledge of God within us, we suffer. I no longer wanted to suffer, neckwise or otherwise.

I was so mind-boggled by the cosmic, time-bending, soul-piercing lessons I was observing that my "school room" became funny. I needed to personalize what I was learning so that I could relate to it personally. I was being treated to all this because of a movie we shot on the remaining mountaintop of the 850,000-year-past "other time." I wanted to know what the movie had to do with it all.

It seemed that just as I thought about personal involvement, a picture came to me. I saw a huge whale of a man in the ocean, drowning. I rescued him with the help of a giraffe! The giraffe bent over and under the water until the man threw his arms around its neck and the animal pulled him up. I brought a boat around, put the man aboard, and guided him toward the main island. He was grateful and subsequently told me that someone else had tried to drown him before.

When we went ashore, he strode with gigantic steps toward a mansion of some kind. On the veranda of the mansion was a big golden chair. I knew it was his. I knew he was the overlord of the mansion. I also knew that the big man was Andy, the director of our film, looking almost exactly the same! Behind him stood a wizened woman. Andy pointed to her and said, "She is the one who tried to drown me before." I looked into her crazed eyes. It was Tyne, the amateur producer of our film! She wanted his golden chair, but Andy had taken possession of it, and the workers who were building a new wing onto the mansion supported him.

He said he was a powerful shaman and needed a golden throne. The wizened woman had no respect for him. Their relationship was extremely competitive. Andy said he was a seashore person. The galactics building the new Atlantis wanted to learn about seashore people. But Andy remained silent and grew feathers in his hair! I was a servant of the galactics, instructed to bring Andy whatever he wished. Andy wanted sex with me. I didn't know what sex was. I teased him on purpose so I could learn. I had no sexual knowing. I was a tall, thin woman who was instructed by the galactics to observe everything.

Andy now jumps off his golden throne and twirls and swirls. He reaches out and pulls me into a twisting swirl. I panic, but my head remains above the swirl. I see many, many stories and lifetimes pass. My higher self says, "Don't go so fast. You miss the meaning." I get caught up in the speeding-up of time. Atlantis is constructed. Gold is everywhere. The galactics tell me they need to turn the gold into powder and take it back to their world. They tell me powdered gold in their skies protects them from the harmful radiation they have incurred for themselves on their home world. I see more tables and chairs being made out of gold—not for show but as a means of storage.

Andy swirls now when he is nervous. I ask for my animals to be brought to us, especially my giraffe. He says I can have anything I want. Many animals now come across the ocean to allow me to pay my respects to them. My arms become very long again. Each animal takes his time on my arms. I am so happy.

The giraffes tell Andy that there is much gold in Africa. The galactics say the frequency and vibration of life in Africa is not comparable with what they need.

All that I was seeing was like a moving dream memory. It felt familiar as well as preposterous. I was living in a panoply of imaginative reality somehow. How could I explain this to anyone? Yes, it was my imagination, but more to the point, I felt I had actually "imagined" my life. In fact I was imagining every moment of my life today. *Images* were necessary to life. Without images there was nothing to see, nothing to relate to. If images were how we defined reality, then imagination created reality. Was that why Einstein said there was nothing more important than imagination? There would be no reality without it? Was I really seeing an ancient past that *really* happened because I was open to my imagined memory, which had actually created events that were real? I didn't want to judge what I was seeing. I wanted to understand it from a personal and experiential point of view. I was familiarizing myself with the moving images of the past as I made the connections with the moving images I experienced making a movie in the present.

With that thought I found myself rising above the antics of Andy with his gold chair and Tyne. Gold was clearly to become the standard for measurement against everything else in the future because another galactic civilization needed to powder it for survival. We would need gold later because materialism would become the surviving humans' new god. Everything was connected.

I rose further above the landmass and could now see Atlantis's connection to other landmass territories. This was when I had my most surprising revelation.

Atlantis was an island continent, magnificent and glorious. Above the floating continent I saw a moon, a second moon. It was made out of crystal. And from the crystal moon extending out to other land territories (later to be countries) were lines of crystal through which power was provided to the people of the other landmasses. I counted the crystal energy lines: there were *eighteen!* Eighteen lines of energy which kept the nine surrounding territories alive and well.

Eighteen! I keeled over, laughing to myself. This was karma I'd never have thought of. Eighteen pages for Flavia C. Face kept our movie going, and eighteen crystal lines in Atlantis kept their Golden Age going. Even I couldn't make that up. Eighteen made the number 9 (1 + 8), which is the number of completion. But what did completion in Atlantis mean? For our movie it meant we could finish the shooting. As I asked myself that question, I fell back to Earth.

I saw Andy in his gold chair. I saw Tyne not knowing how to manage her gold medallion stashes, and I saw Michelos decide to take over the building of some gold pavilions. I saw myself as a very tall, thin giraffe lady! And the galactic star people simply observed us as though they were watching a pitiful movie. They wanted us to be warm and balanced and comfortable with each other. But we weren't. We were squabbling and greedy. My neck hurt again.

I saw the weather react to the chaos among the people. It was as though nature itself followed consciousness. I heard rumblings beneath the earth. The waves of ocean surrounding Atlantis were so chaotic, they rose out of the ocean and into space. Earth, wind, stormy waters, and fire began to disrupt what harmony remained.

I looked up. I saw another galactic nation of travelers observing, watching from their crafts. Somehow I knew they had the power to ease the weather and the chaos below. But instead they were so deeply upset and disappointed at what humans had become, I could feel them decide to let nature take its course.

The chaotic squabbling energy began affecting the crystal moon. It began to crack, sending up sizzling sparks from itself to the nine surrounding lands. The earth rumbled louder and began to undulate as if to try to adjust to a more stable condition of support. I saw the Earth galactics look above for help as though there had been disagreements among them. Did all the star nations agree on what should be the course of Earth humans? No. Perhaps I was seeing the truth of "as above, so below" again. Perhaps nature was reacting in such a colossal way because all life was disagreeing with itself.

The crystal moon was shaking violently. The eighteen lines were shattering and breaking apart. People and galactics were screaming, convulsing with terror. The earth began to explode apart on the Golden Island.

I'll never forget seeing the crystal moon shatter. The violence of light is something I'll always remember. With that explosion the eighteen crystal lines went down, arching toward the earth and burrowing beneath the land. The land arched upward with a gigantic sigh of resignation and came to rest under the ocean. I couldn't measure how much time went by. But I heard in my head, "In a day and one night, it was over. The Golden Age gone."

· · ·

Back to Earth—new reality. Did I give myself a pain in my neck so that I would remember Atlantis? I believe yes, and with the memory, the water decompression therapy, and stem cell injections, my pain disappeared, at least for a little while. Was I warning myself as to what we on this Earth were now creating? I believe yes. My ultimate question became, Does creativity create pain or the other way around? *Again . . . Does creativity create pain or does pain create creativity?*

Whichever you believe to be true (and why not both?), for me the unfortunate truth was that my pain soon came back. I needed to find some other form of treatment that would offer a more lasting solution. Much to my surprise, the answer turned up not only in front of my face but in my face. Literally. It was a problem with my jaw.

I had what is called TMJ. I had heard that term. Temporomandibular joint syndrome refers to a malposition of the respective jaw structures and associated muscles. This condition results in muscle contractions which are a factor in approximately 80 percent of all pain related to back and spine. Some seventy-five million Americans are affected by TMJ syndrome, but only about 5 percent of all TMJ patients are actually diagnosed correctly and treated for their problem. I am one of them. Luckily I found Dr. Bill Wolfe in Albuquerque, New Mexico, a mercury-free dentist who constructed a customized splint that I wear over the top of my lower teeth to alter the way the upper and lower jaw fit together to stabilize my entire spinal column. I wear it twenty-four hours a day except when eating. Thanks to the brilliance of Dr. Wolfe, my long-standing back pain and neck pain, the result of decades of overuse as a dancer, has resolved itself. I'm achieving long-term correction and stability of my spine and enjoying dramatic relief of my chronic pain that I was convinced was going to require surgical intervention. Instead, perhaps the creative expression from my voice had to be balanced with the earth-plane stability of my teeth and muscles in my mouth.

MAKING THE film *Wild Oats* and going through the subsequent neck pain has been the most transformative experience I've ever had. During my time with Atlantis memories, I felt time and stillness and earth and air as real characteristics of me. From spending so much time in the water and remembering the sinking of Atlantis, I find my balance is somewhat off because I'm becoming more aligned with space-time and with slower movements. I wear a giraffe charm around my neck to remind me to slow down. My dreams are the rhythm of nature, peaceful and without conflict because I avoid it at all costs. I'm careful about watching the news because it imprints on my mind—though every now and then I immerse myself in the evening news and pretend I'm watching a horror movie, so it doesn't affect me. I see my past through different eyes. I watch philanthropists giving away money they don't need in order to pay for their sins.

I feel catastrophic change coming. I feel 2017 to 2020 is the turning point. Then there will be a new world. I can't feel how many people will be gone or why. I would like to see what the realign-ment of countries looks like. I've been told by several astrocartographers that the South Pacific and Australia will be safe.

I feel I travel at night. I don't know where. Because I am 98 percent water (as are you!), my consciousness is opening up to truths I can't even imagine. Because water constantly changes, that is the only constant . . . and that is change.

My mind, body, bite, posture, movements, and perspective on everything have changed and continue to do so. Do the star people observe these changes too? I feel I'm preparing for a huge change in understanding. Vibrations and energy will soon be different.

The weather everywhere is speaking to change. Something has definitely shifted. Many coastal regions will be underwater and mountains will slip.

The more I slow down and relax in the water, the more I realize that the energy I feel inside myself defines my existence. I am the designer of what I see, what I'm afraid of, and therefore the level of reality I find myself observing. There can be several realities in the course of an hour, a day, and a year, depending on the energy I stir in myself.

The media, particularly the news, is in alliance with me to design my reality, but then I'm designing the news too.

I feel that I am in alignment with my soul's destiny. I chose to live in unstable yet stimulating times. Perhaps instability stirs the pot and forces us to know better who we are.

We are addicted to physical reality, materialism, and three-dimensional truth. We are the creators of material expression. I'm becoming more and more aware that our third-dimensional level of reality has layers of truth like an onion. Obviously the third dimension is more dense, like our living experience, so dense that we are burdened by it. We are living in a state of layers of fear. Fear lowers our vibrational energy, therefore we become more controllable.

The people who control our material existence on Earth have designed methods of creating fear. We see it every day. I believe it is their designed task to keep us confused and in a state of controlled fear.

I also believe an open heart will become the new brain. Innately we know what is true and what is not. The heart will become the center of intelligence. That is the new reality.

I'm understanding more deeply that nonphysical reality is influencing physical reality. We need to allow our hearts and bodies to be dowsers of the truth. We need to *feel* the truth of our human data. Most of us have been tap-dancing to someone else's tune.

We think that we are free of tyranny. But we are

the tyrannizers of ourselves. I believe the media is mostly giving us senseless entertainment so that we don't bother to think. Something like the Roman games, a distraction from what is actually going on. Unwittingly, perhaps, Hollywood has contributed to mind control with its violent special effects and senseless diversionary scripts. I fear for California's karma.

I feel a deep rift between the power of individual free expression and the power of the collective receivers. I feel the top priority is thought to be material survival and enjoyment. People with these priorities do not want to know the Big Truths.

I believe our dreams are a playground for potential realities. Dreaming and imagination are a fluid state of reality. We shop for a potential reality in a dream state. I love to "reality shop" using the skills of my imagination. We can change the dream if we want to. We can condition our reality. We can rehearse our reality. Therefore, imaginative dreams can build our confidence.

I love to stir my intelligence with imagination.

I believe it is time to turn our ship of state in a more positive direction, using our internal light as a carrier of true information. The entirety of our planet will be riding with a new reality.

AND

I believe we all have star seed in us. I believe it is more than possible that we have the fingerprint of ET star-nation life in our DNA. Perhaps we even have competing star-nation DNA within us, and that's why we continually compete with one another. It is what is called junk DNA because no one yet knows what it's for. But it is far from junk. It is the fundamental stuff of what and who we are.

I will listen to my heart intelligence. I believe it will help me align with the Bigger Truths. I believe that ET star nations are again worried over the future of humanity and unsure about how much they should influence us.

My conclusion: each of us has the innate power to understand and be in control of our own future and destiny by understanding the Big Truth that resides within each of us.

Wild Oats is being edited as I write this. Andy got more money for music. When Tyne heard the score, she cried. Andy forgave her amateurism. Jessica and I have compared experiences. She doesn't think I'm crazy—just highly imaginative. I will probably help sell the movie by promoting it on talk shows, where the hosts will ask me more about ETs and reincarnation and my "mental health." I told Andy I was writing a book about my experiences on the set, and he said, "For the love of God, please tell people you and Jessica both wanted to fuck me!" (Whatever you say, Andy!) I asked him what he was doing about those eighteen new pages that were added to the script—about 144 lines of additional dialogue, it turned out. He told me that he'd done some judicious editing and only about forty lines made it into the final cut. When he was threatened with a lawsuit by our investor, Andy informed him that he had done right by the actress, and then he sent him the footage. Once the investor watched it, he signed off and didn't complain anymore. Any number of possible fates could be in store for this film, from a national theatrical release to being broadcast on a cable television network. Maybe it'll turn up on QVC! That's the crazy state of the movie business these days.

As for me, I will go back to watching the news so I can determine whether I should go live in a secure underground cave with enough supplies for ten thousand years. My choice would be to observe from a star craft and be a record keeper, which would someday make a great movie if we can get financing. I would defer my paycheck yet again. Because it's never really about the money.

POSTSCRIPT

THE FALL of Atlantis was a dramatic event that has for many, many lifetimes plagued and darkened the memories of many of us, who were indeed a part of it. It is time to let it go. Much has been forgotten of the true realm of Atlantis. Many tend to remember only the sad demise, under the Aryan influence of greed and lust for power. It is time to remember the Law of One, the Golden Age of Poseida. For within that Golden Age existed a spiritual matriarchal society which achieved a harmonic state of divine balance, the highest frequency ever achieved upon the Earth plane in what is termed the Golden Age of Atlantis.

The great mass of the surviving inhabitants of Atlantis lived side by side in various populations, each with a chakra system of seven energy centers reflecting the sound system of seven notes in the scale and seven colors in the spectrum of white light.

The Gods who presided over the initial stages of evolution were the Pleiadians, the constellation of Seven Sisters. The Pleiadians have stated many times that our forefathers were their forefathers.

One thing that was true in the time of Atlantis is just as true today: the crystalline energy and indeed the entire mineral kingdom relates to humanity through both physical and etheric means. The realms of the crystalline minerals and humanity are intricately related, so that one is never out of contact or subtle communication with the other. Our physical human bodies contain crystalline particles and a rich array of minerals that are unique to the Earth. That means the harmonic ratios of minerals and crystalline particles that are in both our physical and etheric bodies are maintained in sync with those of the Earth. Thus the resulting frequency ratios of Earth and humanity are held in balance for the well-being and support of humanity individually and en masse.

Every new cosmic era brings with it upshifts and transformations. Both the Earth and indeed mankind are currently experiencing a long-awaited awakening. This metamorphosis includes global warming and all sorts of environmental changes that are quickening around us. A key aspect of the awakening Crystalline Age is a resounding, undeniable call to the crystalline and mineral kingdoms of the Earth to increase the flow of energy radiating from the core of the Earth. Do you hear it? Transformation is at hand.